Hermann Lotze, George Trumbull Ladd

Outlines of Logic

and of Encyclopædia of philosophy

Hermann Lotze, George Trumbull Ladd

Outlines of Logic
and of Encyclopædia of philosophy

ISBN/EAN: 9783337239602

Printed in Europe, USA, Canada, Australia, Japan

Cover: Foto ©Thomas Meinert / pixelio.de

More available books at **www.hansebooks.com**

OUTLINES

OF

L O G I C

AND OF

ENCYCLOPÆDIA OF PHILOSOPHY

DICTATED PORTIONS

OF THE

LECTURES OF HERMANN LOTZE

TRANSLATED AND EDITED BY

GEORGE T. LADD

PROFESSOR OF PHILOSOPHY IN YALE COLLEGE

BOSTON

GINN & COMPANY

1887

J. S. Cushing & Co., Printers, Boston.

EDITOR'S PREFACE.

THIS volume is a translation of the second German edition of Lotze's "Outlines of Logic and Encyclopædia of Philosophy," which appeared in 1885. The second edition differed from the earlier one chiefly in the abbreviation of certain parts of the Encyclopædia of Philosophy. The matter thus omitted consisted largely either of opinions expressed elsewhere in the Philosophical Outlines, or of a somewhat special criticism of certain views of Schelling, Fichte, and Herbart. It has therefore been thought best to take for translation the more recent but somewhat less voluminous German text.

Although Lotze dealt with the subject of Logic in a large and technical treatise, which constituted one of the two volumes of his System of Philosophy, completed by him before his death, it must be said that his contributions to it are perhaps less distinctive and valuable than those to any other of the several branches of philosophy upon which he wrote and lectured. Notwithstanding this, his views upon some important topics under the general subject will be found very suggestive and valuable. This seems

to me particularly true of the chapter on the "Formation of Concepts." There can be little doubt that
the distinction between the association of mental
images and the definitely logical processes of the
mind is far too little drawn and too loosely held by
certain English writers on Logic.

Part Second, which treats of the "Encyclopædia
of Philosophy," so-called, will be found to contain a
number of articles which throw considerable additional light upon the author's general philosophical
position. His peculiar doctrine of "Values," as distinguished from a knowledge of what is necessitated
or real, his view of the general method of philosöphy,
and of the relation in which the Theory of Cognition
stands to the whole of Metaphysics, and his attitude
toward philosophical Scepticism and Criticism, will
doubtless receive some elucidation from the careful
study of these sections.

A first draught of the translation of §§ 6–38 of the
Pure Logic was made by John F. Crowell, graduate
student of Philosophy in Yale University, 1885–86.
The rest of the work upon the volume is by my
own hand. With this sixth number of the series
of Lotze's Philosophical Outlines, I regard my task
as completed.

GEORGE T. LADD.

NEW HAVEN, March, 1887.

TABLE OF CONTENTS.

———•◦•———

I. LOGIC.

—◆—

INTRODUCTION.

§ 1. According to the combination in which the external stimuli happen to act upon us, there arise within us manifold ideas, simultaneous or successive, which do not always have an interior coherence that agrees with the nature of their *Content*. And, further, since memory and recollection retain and reproduce these ideas in the same connections which they had at their origin, certain ideas that are quite foreign to each other and without any interior coherence, very often appear in our mental train in a connection which, although it is matter of fact, is without any real reason.

§ 2. Besides, perception by the senses affords us the impressions of at least one sense, — namely, that of sight, — in an arrangement with reference to each other which has *space-form ;* and this arrangement is not, like the connection referred to above, a merely accidental coexistence of the single colored points, but undoubtedly depends upon the peculiar nature of what is perceived. Nevertheless, we do not call this 'thought' but 'intuition,' — and for the very reason that, while we discover the arrangement of the single points to be unalterable, we yet perceive it as a bare matter of fact without understanding the *reasons* on account of which each point has its position toward others.

§ **3.** We are accustomed to distinguish *thought* both from the aforesaid train of ideas and also from such process of intuition, as a higher and self-cohering activity, which elaborates, shapes, and connects the material of ideas furnished by both of the others. Its essential tendency can be expressed as follows ; — that the thinking spirit is not satisfied to receive the ideas simply in those combinations in which what is accidental to the physical mechanism has brought them to it.   Thought is rather of the nature of a continuous 'critique,' which the spirit practises upon the material of the train of ideas, when it separates the ideas whose connection is not founded upon some such justification for the combination as lies in the very nature of their content ; while it not only combines those ideas whose content permits or requires some connection, but likewise reconstructs their combination in some new form of apprehension and expression, from which the justification of this connection admits of being discerned.

§ 4. If we assume (not as a positive assertion, but only as an aid to the exposition of the subject) that the animals, although possessing the train of ideas alluded to, do not possess thought specifically ; then the distinction between these two achievements would lie in what follows.

In the animal, with the idea of the stick when swung, the idea of the pain that follows thereupon is connected ; and the renewal of the first alone is sufficient to reproduce in anticipation the second also, and to determine the behavior of the animal in some purposeful way.

Practically, therefore, the animal obtains fairly well from the mere association of ideas the same service as though it had, by thinking in the strict meaning of the word, expressed its experience in the form of judgments and conclusions, as follows : ' The stick strikes — the stroke smarts — therefore, etc.' Still in each of these logical judgments there would be involved an apprehension of the state of the case quite other and more profound than is involved in such mere association. That is to say, when we apprehend the stick as the *subject* or *cause* from which the stroke proceeds, we do not merely repeat the psychological fact that the ideas of the two *occur* in connection, but likewise express the adjunct thought that both belong together by an inner bond uniting their content, — in this case, by a causal relation. The same thing is true in all cases, as will subsequently be shown in particular.

Thought, therefore, carries the merely subjective association of ideas — that is, their mere occurrence together in consciousness as a matter of fact — back to principles that govern the objective synthesis of their content.

§ 5. In order that the process of thinking may be able to accomplish such an achievement, it must have in its possession the principles for it, — that is to say, certain universal rules or grounds of right, according to which, in general, the content of different ideas may, or may not, be capable of connection. Or, to express the same thing in another way : if we are to be able to distinguish truth and untruth, then there must exist within us some absolutely valid and universal standard determining what is permissible, and what is not permissible, as to the connections of ideas. Moreover, the general principles contained in it must stand in a very close connection with the presuppositions which we are compelled to make concerning the nature and the reciprocal relations of all 'Things.'

These latter we are accustomed to style *metaphysical* principles.   And, accordingly, a near relationship would exist between logical and metaphysical
truths.   This Introduction is not the place to treat
this relationship exhaustively; the following remark
is sufficient at this point.

We assume that the process of thinking is *determined* so as to lead to the knowledge of the true
nature of 'Things.'   Now every means must be
directed, on the one hand toward the object which
it is to work out, and on the other hand toward
the nature of that which is to employ it.   On this
account, the forms and the laws also, in which and
according to which thought connects the ideas, must
be such that by means of them the knowledge of
truth can be conclusively attained; but they need
not be such that the ideas shall directly copy the
essence of the 'Things' themselves.   The rather,
since it is *man* who, by means of them, is to arrive
at the truth, must they attach themselves to the
nature and stand-point of man ; and accordingly they
must have peculiarities which are comprehensible
only from this fact, and not from the nature of the
'Things' which are to be known.

In other words (to answer, at least in a preliminary way, a question which is not to be exhaustively
treated in this place) : The forms and laws of thought,

with which we are to become acquainted, have neither a 'merely formal' nor a 'perfectly real' significance. They are neither *mere* results of the organization of our subjective spirit, without respect to the nature of the objects to be known, nor are they direct *copies* of the nature and reciprocal relations of these objects. They are rather 'formal' and 'real' at the same time. That is to say, they are those subjective modes of the connection of our thoughts which are necessary to us, if we are by thinking to know the objective truth.

FIRST PRINCIPAL DIVISION.

PURE LOGIC.

First Principal Division.

—◆—

PURE LOGIC.

—◆—

CHAPTER I.

THE FORMATION OF CONCEPTS.

§ 6. It is well known that most of the operations of thought consist in acts connecting together different simple ideas. Wherever, then, some such 'connection' is spoken of, the question at once arises, How must the simple elements themselves be formed in order to be able to enter at all into the connection designated? Out of purely spherical elements it is impossible to make a coherent structure. That can be done only by means of prismatic elements which present to each other surfaces that are definitely laid out. Just so, from mere impressions, in so far as they are nothing more than our affections (moods, that is, of our feeling), no logical connection is to be established; but each individual impression, in order to be capable, in the logical sense, of being combined with another into a *thought*, must be already apprehended by the spirit in such a quite definite form as renders this combination possible.

§ **7.** This, the first work of logical thought, becomes most distinctly apparent to us in the circumstance, that almost all languages divide the whole stock of the content of ideas into definite, formally different classes; and that even those languages which do not distinguish externally this difference between substantives, adjectives, verbs, etc., still cherish, in forming each one of their words, the adjunct thought, that its content must be conceived of either substantively, as something in itself valid, permanent, independent of every other; or adjectively, as quality dependent and presupposing some other to which it adheres; or verbally, as a movement or relation passing between different contents. In the first place, by means of these forms in which they are cast by the act of thinking, ideas become elements of a thought; and, like the prismatic stones in the comparison made above, they turn toward one another definite surfaces which allow a connection in the logical sense. So long, on the other hand, as ideas are only different modes of being apprehended in our consciousness, although

they can, of course, like tones in music, be signifi-
cantly connected with one another in other ways
(in this case, *æsthetically*), yet as such no *thought*
arises from them.

§ 8. The next question seems necessarily to be,
How must thought always proceed in order to accomplish this arrangement of any content whatever
in one of these forms taken by the parts of speech?
Since the question relates quite generally to every
content, simple as well as composite, this *second*
logical act of thought must consist in a very simple process which can occur in both cases.

Now it does consist in the following : — As often
as language forms a word for some content, which
is to be ascribed to this particular content and to it
alone, it necessarily expresses therewith the presupposition that this content is something which holds
good of itself, is identical with itself, and different
from others ; that, on this very account; it is able
to bear a name of its own. That is, when the secondary thought, which occurs along with the act
of thinking, forms in speech a word for a thing
(that is, apart from speech, when it *fixes* some content, and distinguishes it from others), it consists
particularly in this, that it conceives of it as a whole
which in itself belongs together, and as thus belonging together is marked off from every other.

Expression in speech permits this act to be man-
ifest in different classes of words with different
degrees of distinctness.   An adjective, as 'blue,'
expresses least of this logical import. Verbs signify by means of their ending, that the content
indicated by them is thought of as a unity in a definite sense, — namely, in that of the verbal relation.
In the case of substantives, certain languages make
it most palpable that the content designated should
be thought of as something identical with itself,
exclusive, one and entire, by means of the prefixed
article.

§ 9. This logical form of the 'idea' (so we will
call this second act of thought) accordingly apprehends its content, be it simple or composite, only in
such a way that it comes in general to be regarded
as *unity* or as *totality*.

In reference to simple content, that which admits
of being realized at all stands highest.   For example ; the impressions, 'blue,' 'sweet,' 'warm,' cannot
undergo any other logical elaboration than that of
being apprehended as having a content which is
identical with itself, different from others, and of
course adjective in its nature.

For the composite content, on the other hand, this
form of the idea which asserts in a general way

nothing more than that its parts belong together,
without rendering cognizable the kind, the ground,
and the rule of the same, is an unsatisfactory mode
of apprehension ; although we very frequently cannot
get beyond this in the ordinary course of thought.[1]
The words 'nature,' 'life,' 'state,' 'government,'
indicate for the majority of men nothing but the
consciousness that in every case a manifold of phenomena and events is united into a totality ; without
their being able to specify the definite plan, the laws
and the forces, according to which and through
which this totality is produced. These same words,
however, will indicate a *higher* apprehension of their
content, a '*concept*' of the same, in case, besides the
bare fact that the parts of the content belong together, some *reason* for the latter is also thought.

§ 10. Now it is this principle of 'belonging together' which thought seeks to discover ; since it
has regard either to that which, in several ideas
that differ from each other, appears as common
and homogeneous (the *universal*) ; or to that which,
throughout all changes of one and the same con-

---

[1] Especially useful kinds of expression for anything thought of merely
in the form of idea, are such as these : in the Greek the neuter plural, —
τὰ φυσικά, τὰ ἠθικά, τὰ πολιτικά; in the German, compounds
with ... '*wesen*,' — *Münzwesen, Zollwesen, Heerwesen*, etc.

tent, continually remains homogeneous (the *constant*). For there naturally seems to lie in both, somewhat which coheres together more firmly and legitimately than the other changing and heterogeneous marks, and which, just for these marks, composes the principle of their coexistence and determines the kind of their combination.

Should a composite content be thought, however, in such a way that somewhat universal or constant, but distinct from the sum-total of its 'marks,' be thought along with it as the determining law on which that whole circle of marks is dependent ; then is that content thought in the form of a *concept.*

The name 'linden,' 'oak,' and the like, moreover, designates for the ordinary course of thought a content apprehended in accordance with a concept. For every one conceives of the general image of 'tree,' or the still more general image of 'plant,' as the outline, the schema, or the norm, according to which all parts of the afore-mentioned individual ideas are bound together into a whole. So, too, all *nomina propria* of persons are real concepts. 'Alcibiades,' or 'Napoleon,' never means merely a totality of parts ; but both are explained and conceived of under the accompanying universal mental image of ' man.'

§ 11. Very rarely will such a general image admit of being produced from several comparable individual ideas through the retention of their marks that are completely alike, and the simple omission of those unlike. For the marks of ideas are not wont to be alike and unlike, but *similar* and *dissimilar*. If indeed we should merely retain what little is precisely alike, we should arrive at a meaningless universal which would sustain a relation of complete indifference toward the omitted constituents, and not that of a principle regulating them.

But in fact we do not so proceed. The comparison of several bodies does not result in the general image of body, — because one is blue, hard, elastic, light, and the other is yellow, soft, ductile, and heavy, — by omitting all of these properties ; as though the idea of ' body ' would have any meaning at all regardless of ' color,' ' cohesion,' and ' weight.' Of these dissimilar marks the comparison omits merely what is different, but retains what is common to them (for example, in this case, ' color in general,' ' weight in general ') ; and it combines these general marks themselves into the desired general image of a body, to which it is therefore quite essential that it should have some color, some cohesion, some weight, or other.

§ 12. The ordinary theory of logic is accustomed simply to teach that, from comparable individual ideas (*notiones speciales*) we ascend to the more universal one (*notio generalis*) by 'abstracting' from the unlike marks (*notae*) of the former, and retaining only the like ones. This theory adds the statement, therefore, that the content (*materia complexus*) of a general idea is 'poorer,' that is, can count fewer marks than that of the particular ones out of comparison of which it arose.

The foregoing remark must at all events be improved upon to this extent, that each universal has exactly so many marks, which it is indispensable should be thought together, as belong to the individuals corresponding to it. Nevertheless, while all these marks are perfectly defined in the particular or in the individual, as respects both kind and quantity ; in the universal, certain general or undefined marks have taken the place of many of them. The universal, as compared with the particular, is therefore poorer in defined marks, but not poorer in marks in general.

§ 13. We distinguish, therefore, two different kinds of universals. In the first place, there is the aforesaid general image, through the entrance of which into the group of marks belonging to an idea, this idea is itself raised to a concept ; and, besides this,

those universal marks out of whose connection together the general image itself arises.

These latter, the universal marks, in the simplest
case require no special logical work of thought for
their origin, but arise out of the immediate impression without our logical assistance. That 'green,'
'blue,' 'red,' for example, have something in common,
is a matter of immediate experience ; and although
this common possession may not admit of being separated by a logical operation from that by which
these impressions are *distinguished;* still the name
'color' points to this as to the something experienced
as common. So, too, differences of magnitude are
immediately perceived as true; and the general name
of magnitude expresses, side by side with these distinctions, the common characteristic.

In this manner there arise from the consideration
of the different marks, which are presented in the
individual ideas, the general marks as the elements
out of which the aforesaid general image is then
composed ; and the latter holds good for those
individual ideas as a common type comprising
them all.

§ 14. For the formation of a *'concept'* it is not
sufficient that its general marks, nor indeed for the
formation of the 'idea,' is it enough that its indi-

vidual marks, be merely present in general; but the essential thing is their mode of combination. No idea, and no concept, consists of a mere summation of marks in such a way that every first one should enter into combination with every second one just as the second with every third; but in the universal the marks limit, define, or determine one another in such manifold and characteristic ways, that a first one is connected with the second otherwise than the second is connected with the third, or the third with the fourth.

In the case of mere ideas which only combine marks in general into a totality, without logically characterizing the way in which they belong to-gether, the intuitions of time and space take the place of such strictly logical work. Through these intuitions we then know in what way, for in-stance, the distinctive marks of an animal — color, skin, head, swiftness, etc. — are to be brought to-gether and combined. If, on the other hand, we form an abstract concept of 'motion,' for example, and designate it as 'constant change of place,' then it is seen that no one of these three marks is thought as of like species with the other; but, strictly speak-ing, simply the general idea of 'change,' in so far as it is restricted by reference to the idea of 'place,' and through the mark belonging to it is defined as 'constant,' forms the content of the concept of motion.

The general image which arises out of the comparison of several individual ideas is formed, not simply when the general marks are put in the place of the particular, but also when a general mode of connection corresponding to them is put in the place of the particular modes of connection among the marks.

The general mental image 'metal' — for instance — connects together the general marks of 'color,' 'weight,' etc., in a form, or according to a scheme, of which the modes of combination are only particular examples, wherein gold combines the color yellow, *its* specific gravity, etc., copper the color red, and *its* specific gravity, etc.

§ 15. To recapitulate the foregoing ; we give the name of *'concept'* to an idea whenever, in addition to its group of marks, a universal is thought along with it as an explanatory law. 'Gold' or 'Caius' is thus thought as concept, in so far as the marks of both are regulated by the general schemata, 'metal' and 'man,' respectively.

The universal itself, by whose entrance into it the idea becomes the concept, is not necessarily nor always itself thought as concept, but frequently only as idea. It is then, indeed, concept only when its own marks also are not merely thought in general as a whole belonging together, but as combined by means of a new universal in accordance with some definite scheme.

There are accordingly just as much individual, singular concepts (*notiones singulares*) — like all names of persons, for instance — as there are universal concepts (*notiones generales*) in manifold gradations.

The name of *higher* general concept is given to that one, which is thought as an explanatory schema in addition to the marks of another concept, which latter is then the *lower* of the two.

It is then said that the content (*materia*) of the higher general concept (*genus*) is 'contained' in the content of the lower (*species*) ; that is, that all the marks which are essential to the genus occur also in the species. But, conversely, the content of the species is not entirely contained in that of the genus ; but the former possesses, besides the particular marks of the latter, certain ones peculiar to it as species. On this matter a corrective remark is made above (§ 12).

It is further said — and rightly, too — that each higher general concept occurs in a greater number of kinds or individual concepts (or holds good of them) than the lower concept. The name of 'extent' (*ambitus*) is given to the number of these lower concepts, of which the higher holds good. And since to the latter there is ascribed, as previously remarked, a smaller number of marks or smaller content (*materia complexus*) ; therefore it is said that "the extent and the content of two concepts are in inverse ratio to each other" : the one poorer in content — that is, the more general — commands a greater aggregate of individual cases ; the one richer in content occurs in fewer kinds, perhaps only in a single individual.

According to the foregoing, this proposition would correctly run thus : A concept with clearly defined marks is always individual. In case it has undefined or general marks besides the defined ones, then with the number of the undefined marks (or, conversely, with the number of the defined ones), the number of cases increases in which it is valid, — that is, its extent.

§ 16. Two relations of subordination, since they are essentially different logically, are to be held as excluding each other. That is to say, every concept can be ranked in respect to one part of it, under its higher concept of species, — for example, 'gold' (**G**) under 'metal' (**M**) ; in respect to another part, under

any one of its marks at pleasure, — for example,
'gold' (**G**) under 'fusible' (**F**).

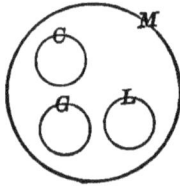

Fig. 1.

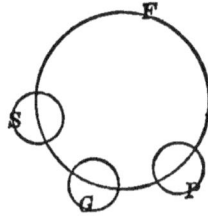

Fig. 2.

The first of the foregoing relations (Fig. 1.) is
called *subordination*. In this case the whole nature
of **G** is included in the universal **M**, in such a manner that there is in **G** no part, no mark and no combination of marks, which may not be essentially
comprehended by means of the universal principle
M; for example, the 'yellow' of gold is a certain
lustrous yellow peculiar to the metal, which does
not occur otherwise. Within this **M**, finally, **G** is
found 'co-ordinated' with its natural kindred (copper,
lead, silver, — **C**, **L**, — etc.) ; that is, it stands in the
same logical relation to **M** with all the rest of them.

The other species of arrangement of one concept
under another (Fig. 2) is called *subsumption*. Here
G touches upon the universal concept **F** with only
one part of its content; the remaining parts of its
content lie outside **F** and are not defined by **F**. Besides, **G** (gold) is found in this case to be co-ordi-

nated, in reference to **F** (fusible), not merely with its own related species, but also with other concepts of content altogether heterogeneous (sugar, pitch, sulphur, — **S**, **P**, — etc.).

§ **17.** If we ascend by continued abstraction to more and more general concepts, we shall, according to a frequent assertion, reach one single highest general concept, — that of the 'thinkable.' Such an abstraction, however, would only be performed through *subsumption* (Fig. 2), if the concept should have entirely let go of the characteristic content of the concepts, and confined itself simply to a common mark through which its content is *not* defined.

If we proceed by way of *subordination*, then it is found that our system of concepts does not terminate in one point, but in several independent points. The substantive concepts lead to one highest concept of *Being;* the verbal to that of *Becoming;* the adjective to that of *Property, etc.;* and there is absolutely no concept still higher, to which these fundamental concepts may be referred as to a common principle of their content. As for the rest, it is obvious, — and the reason why it must be so needs no explanation, — that these fundamental concepts are nothing more than the *meanings* belonging to the different parts of speech.

CHAPTER II.

A. *Preliminary Remarks and the Customary Division of Judgments.*

§ 18. The consideration of the subject up to this point leads to a new problem. In the concept we have distinguished the universal and the special circle of marks. Concerning the reciprocal relations of these two members we had, however, only expressions characteristic of like species. The universal served us only as a nucleus, as a normative principle, as a rule for the disposition and combination of the marks. The question now arises; what this means, when taken strictly, and what power the universal can exercise over the marks, and in what way.

We consequently seek for an explanation of the relation of the two members to each other. Every assertion which thought can utter on this question, and by means of which it can answer the same, must consequently take this form; that it connects two members **S** and **P** through the affirmation of a definite mode of relation **X**. This is essentially

the form of a proposition or a judgment, in which
S is subject, P is predicate, and X copula between
the two.

§ 19. The ground of the fact that different impressions belong together, however, we have sought,
not merely in somewhat universal which is common
to the different impressions, but likewise in somewhat constant which appertains to one and the
same content of the idea, while it experiences
changes in other respects by accession or diminution
of its marks. This relation, too, of an unchanging
nucleus, which is at once the ground of the possibility of the changing marks and the law of their
connection, requires a similar investigation. We
must know how any P can 'adhere' to an S, and
how it is possible that it disappears again and
another mark, P', occupies its place, — and every
assertion on this matter must bear the form of
the *judgment*.

§ 20. Apart from such systematic coherency, the
doctrine of judgment may be introduced as follows : — In the train of ideas it must frequently
occur that, in the first place, two impressions a
and b, which have for us become united in part
(as, for example, the shape of a tree and its green

color), are apprehended as a whole whose distinguishable parts are not actually distinguished, because all reason for it is wanting. If now, by a second experience, the tree is shown without leaves, then, in a third instance in which it is again seen to be green, the two ideas of its shape and color will no longer form an undivided whole in the same naïve way; on the contrary, the recollection of their being separable will keep them apart from each other; and therewith arises the idea of two impressions which are combined, instead of that of one impression, in which there is no inner difference.

This process of the simultaneous association and separation of two ideas without doubt takes place in animals also. It supplies for them the place of the logical judgment of human thought; yet it is not such itself, but only the occasion of a judgment. If we, for instance, affirm in judgment, 'the tree is green' or 'is not green,' then we *interpret* the coexistence of separable ideas and do not simply express over again the fact of such coexistence. When we conceive of the tree as subject (or in this case as substance) and the predicate green as attribute or accident, we point to that inner connection in which, according to our view, the property stands related to the 'Thing' or the accident to its subject, as in each case constituting the legitimate ground according to which both of the ideas 'tree' and 'green' do not merely *exist* together, but *belong* together precisely as they are together, — to wit, as separable yet conjoined.

§ **21.** The essential part of a judgment is, then, precisely this secondary thought which the process of thinking has, when it connects subject and predicate in definite form. As many as are the essentially different points of view, grounds, or models, to which this process of thought rightly refers the combination of **S** and **P**, — that is, as many as the essentially different meanings of the copula actually are ; so many are the essentially different logical forms of the judgment which are to be systematically developed later on.

We previously made mention of a classification of the judgment usually given, — namely that by Kant. According to him, every judgment must at the same time be determined in *four* different respects, and must in each of these have one of the three mutually exclusive forms ; namely, is —

1) According to *quantity* either universal or particular or singular.

2) According to *quality* it is either affirmative or negative or limitative.

3) According to *relation*, — that is, the meaning of

the connection between **S** and **P** — either categorical or hypothetical or disjunctive.

4) According to *modality*, — that is, the relation of the whole content to actuality — either problematic or assertory or apodictic.

§ **22.** These differences are not of equal value:

1) To begin with, in the three quantitative forms:

This **S** is **P**,

Some **S** are **P**,

All **S** are **P**, —

the kind of combination between **S** and **P** is entirely the same; and they differ simply in respect to the number of the subjects, and consequently in respect to the material, to which this entirely identical connection is extended. Accordingly, although the quantitative differences remain of great importance for other purposes, — for example, the drawing of conclusions from judgments, — they are nevertheless not essentially different steps in the development of the *judgment as such.*

2) As to what further concerns the qualitative forms, it is obvious that the affirmative and the negative judgment,

S is **P**,

S is *not* **P**,

must understand the kind of combination that takes

place between S and P, in the same manner.
For the negative judgment could not be the exact
opposite of the affirmative, if it did not deny precisely what the latter asserts. This judgment is therefore fitly presented in such a way that, to one entirely
identical thought of a combination of S and P, there
is added the two secondary judgments; — it is true,
or it is not true. They differ then in their content
very essentially, but not in their form. — The limitative judgment should attach a negative predicate to
S by means of a positive copula, and so have the form
S is non-P.
On the other hand, it must be kept in mind that
non-P is a definite idea and not of any use at all to the
predicate, only in those cases where it does not merely
indicate that which is in general not P, but that
which is co-ordinated with P under a higher general
concept, and therefore has a meaning of its own, —
as for instance, 'not-round' in so far as it must still
always have some form, either straight or angular
and the like. If, on the contrary, non-P is intended
to comprehend everything that is simply not P in
general, — for example, the 'not-round' is to include,
besides the angular, things like the 'bitter,' the
'future,' the 'cheap,' etc. ; then non-P is no longer
an idea at all, such as could be apprehended and
given to some subject S as its predicate. The

attempt to do this invariably has in time this issue, that S is excluded from the circle of the predicate **P**, and the judgment consequently, according to its meaning, is *negative*.

3) The third distinction, that according to relation, is of such essential significance that it is passed by here in order to be thoroughly examined later.

4) The differences of modality, likewise, have no essentially *logical* value ; since the possibility of the combination of S and **P** in the problematical judgment, and its necessity in the apodictic judgment, is expressed only by means of the auxiliary verbs,

S may be P,

S must be P.

They are both therefore, after all, properly speaking, only assertory judgments ; that is, they affirm, exactly as does the strictly assertory judgment,

S is P,

an actuality — in the former case, that of possibility ; in the latter, that of necessity.

But neither of the two admits of being brought forward immediately as a consequence of the peculiar mode of relation of S and **P**. This kind of modality, therefore, belongs to the content, but not to the logical form of the judgment ; and there may be set beside it yet many other forms of precisely equal rank ; as, for instance, **S** *should* be **P**, **S** *ought* to be **P**, **S** *will* be **P**, etc. Now, in what way the judgments are capable of expressing, by means of their form, at the same time a claim to the possibility, actuality, or necessity of their content, will be shown by what follows.

B. System of the Forms of Judgment.

§ 23. In the classification of the forms of judgment, we start from the point of view that thought should declare itself as to how it conceives of the coherency of that previously so-called '*nucleus*' of an idea with its own circle of marks ; or, in other words, of an **S** with **P**. Every such declaration will be expressed by a separate form of judgment ; and the series of the forms of judgment must therefore form a series of increasingly better attempts at the complete and adequate expression of the aforesaid relation between **S** and **P**.

§ 24. The simplest form of judgment is the impersonal. In the propositions, 'It lightens,' 'It thunders,' etc., the whole content of the judgment is completely contained in the predicate. The indefinite pronoun 'it' adds nothing thereto, but formally marks the place of the concept of the subject, which is missing. But just this alone — that the process of thinking is not satisfied with the bare reproduction

of the simple content which stands in the predicate,
that it consequently does not employ for its expression the infinitive 'to thunder,' but inflects the word
and joins it as predicate to the 'it' — proves most
evidently this fundamental necessity of analyzing
every content of an idea into two component parts,
the one of which is the regulative principle, and the
other the phenomenon dependent on it. Of course,
this requirement is here only formally satisfied. For
the case does not admit of specifying any subject,
with complete content, to which the phenomenon is
attached. We are, therefore, under the necessity
of joining the phenomenon taken as predicate to
itself taken as subject.[1]

§ 25. The next advance must consist in this, that
the separation of the ideated content in S and P,
which is here only indicated, is brought to comple-

---

[1] According to their modality, the impersonal judgments are naturally
assertory; that is, affirmations of actuality. In the *natural* process of
thinking, they uniformly express perceptions. The 'it' in the subject is,
according to its content, either nothing more than the predicate, or, if it is
to be distinguished from it, is only the thought of the universal Being, which
in the different phenomena is defined now in one way and now in another.
One might therefore say, instead of 'it lightens,' 'the Being is [now] light-
ening,' or conversely, 'the lightning is.' That is to say, it is possible to
convert the impersonal judgments into existential propositions, in which
'to be' is the predicate. Such conversion is, however, an artificial work of
the schools. The natural process of thought never apprehends the individual phenomenon as subject and the Being as predicate, but only universal Being as subject and the phenomenon as a single predicate of the same.

tion by the rise of a special conception of the subject as different from the predicate.

This gives the so-called categorical form of judgment, **S** is **P**, in which **P** is unconditionally and without further justification asserted of **S** (κατηγορεῖται, Aristotle). The only available justification of this connection, — namely, that it takes place according to the type of the relation between ' *Thing*' and property, Substance and attribute (Kant) — does not suffice; since, metaphysically considered, this relation itself is not a perfectly clear truth but an enigma.

We can then distinguish two kinds of this judgment. One, the so-called *analytic*, connects with **S** a **P** which is itself included in the very concept of **S** ; as, for example, 'Gold is heavy.' For the concept of 'gold' is not a completed product of thought until it includes the mark 'heavy.' Accordingly, this judgment, strictly speaking, simply asserts that, when we think the concept **S**, we think along with it that of **P** as a constituent part of it. But how the content of the **P** as a matter of fact adheres to the content of the **S**, in such a way that, just in order to think **S**, we must think **P** along with it, — *this* the form of judgment does not explain, but merely asserts as a fact.

The second kind, the so-called synthetic or historical judgment, connects S with a P that does not lie thus within the concept, and consequently is a changeable mark of it; for example, 'Cæsar fled,' 'The dog is mad.' Here it is far less clear through the form of the judgment, by what right two conceptions which stand in no constant relation are brought into such a relation. But here also the combination is expressed unconditionally as a fact to be taken for granted.

§ **26.** On occasion of this doubt arising and as the ground of it, the first universal law of thought comes to consciousness: The law of identity and of contradiction (*Principium identitatis et contradictionis*).

Its simplest logical expression is this: In a categorical judgment of the form S is P it is absolutely forbidden to combine unconditionally, as subject and predicate, two different concepts S and P, whatever they may be. The rather can only the *two* propositions 'S is S' and 'P is P' always hold good; but never 'S is P' or 'P is S.'

The usual form of the proposition 'A = A', (Proposition of identity), and the negative 'A not = non-A' (Proposition of contradiction) both express this simple truth, that every thinkable content is equal to itself and different from every other one.

This simple logical meaning of the proposition

must without fail be distinguished from other theorems, partly true and partly doubtful, which, although they spring from the application of the universal logical proposition of identity, still do so only from its application to a definite real content, and are not on a par with the proposition itself. For example, that every 'Thing' is like itself, or that it is unchangeably like itself, is a *metaphysical* proposition which arises from an application of the logical proposition of identity to the concept of the 'Existent.' The logical proposition itself says nothing at all of 'Things.' It is also valid of events that happen, of conditions that take place, of the real as truly as of the unreal. And of all of them it merely says, that to be is to be, the changeable is changeable, the contradictory is contradictory, the impossible is impossible.

§ **27**. Briefly expressed, then, the proposition of identity asserts, that all categorical judgments of the form 'S is P' are false and inadmissible. Now since such judgments nevertheless very frequently occur, and we are sufficiently convinced of their admissibility, their defect can only consist in the fact, that they express a correct sentiment with formal imperfection. And an interpretation of them must be given by which they can be justified before the law of identity.

Attempts were first made at this in such a way that a distinction was made between predicates *compatible*, and those *incompatible* with the subject. And as no one is capable of knowing from purely logical laws, what **P** is compatible with what **S**, therefore the general meaning was given to the proposition of identity: Of two incompatible predicates only one can belong to one subject. This proposition, correct in itself, nevertheless does not justify the categorical judgment at all. For it in turn always presupposes that an **S** *can* be a **P**. And it is just this which the proposition of identity forbids without exception, no matter in what the **P** may consist.

Another attempt at justification makes prominent the fact, that in the proposition '**S** is **P**' (gold is yellow), **S** and **P** are by no means interpreted as identical in such a way that the one could be substituted for the other, and consequently the judgment be inverted and read, 'yellow is gold.' Between both, the rather, another relation is maintained which is fitly expressed by '**S** has **P**.' Against this relation, that a mark is 'had' by its subject, or a property by the 'Thing,' the proposition of identity raises no protest. This view, also, although it alludes to something that is quite true, does not reach the end desired. It indeed removes the difficulty of combining with S the content of P which differs from S. But it does not explain how it is possible to combine with S the conception of 'having' (although it does explain *what* is had). For since S is obviously able to 'have' as well as 'not have,' 'having' is itself in turn a predicate determination differing from that of the mere Being of S; and the question recurs concerning *this* predicate, how it is compatible with S. The proposition of identity simply says, S is S. Every proposition, S *has* something or other, therefore declares something different of the S, from the mere proposition that it *is* S; and, consequently, is itself defective as respects the proposition of identity.

§ 28. The solution of the above-mentioned difficulty lies approximately in this, that all categorical judgments are according to their intent and meaning identical but express this intent in a formally imperfect way ; since they allude to only single parts, sometimes of the true subject and sometimes of the true predicate.

For example ; 'Gold is yellow' means (as in Latin the neuter of the adjective shows) the same as 'gold is yellow gold,' — an observation which has been for a very long time expressed in such a way that, in the judgment, the subject is not merely defined or determined by the predicate, but likewise the predicate by the subject. 'Yellow,' for instance, means here not simply 'yellow in general,' but in particular 'gold-yellow.'

The proposition 'Some men are black' is ambiguous in German. The Latin '*Nonnulli homines sunt nigri*' shows that in the predicate *homines* is to be supplied. Now '*nonnulli homines*' and '*nigri homines*' undoubtedly seem to be two entirely different conceptions. But still it is not meant, that every 'some' men you please, taken out of the totality, so far as they are 'some,' would be 'black'; but we understand a perfectly definite 'some,' — namely, the negroes. Therefore **S** and **P** are wholly identical as respects content, and only indicate in different ways, that in **P** one instance (**S**) is characterized as part of a more general concept by means of its properties.

Finally, the historical judgments — for example, 'the dog drinks,' 'Cæsar crossed the Rubicon' — that is, all which express particular facts but not uniformly valid relations, have for their true subject, not the concept *simpliciter*, which appears at this place, but always such concept together with a multitude of secondary ideas, sometimes suppressed and sometimes indicated, which we will call **X**; so that they properly have the form '$S + X = P$.' Thus in the foregoing examples, it is not the universal dog which is drinking, but some specific one whose differences from other dogs are not pointed out; but which, when we add in thought all its peculiarities, — for instance, its temperament, the nourishment it has previously had, its thirst, and the temperature in which it lives — is then exactly the same dog which in the predicate cannot be thought of as any other than the dog which is drinking.

These secondary ideas **X**, in the customary expression of categorical judgments, are wont to be designated mostly through the particular quantity of the subject : for example, '*this* **S** is **P**'; 'some **S** are **P**'; or by particular denotation of the predicate, as '**S** is *sometimes* **P**'; '**S** *was* **P**'; and the like. On this account we give to this entire grade the form of the '*particular judgments.*'

§ **29.** What these particular judgments indicate, is more expressly alluded to in the more developed form of the hypothetical judgments. Here the accessory circumstances, which are in the previous form suppressed or only indicated, are designated in some antecedent proposition as the condition which must be fulfilled, if **P** as predicate is to be capable of being adjoined to the concept of the subject **S**.

The simplest form will be this : If to **S** an **X** be

added, then S has the predicate P; that is, antecedent and consequent propositions have the same concept of the subject, which in the antecedent is
completed by means of X so as to become the real
subject to which in the consequent P must be
attached. In the usage of thought, other forms may
arise by suppression of the middle terms; for example, 'If R is an X, then S is a P.' Nevertheless they
always depend upon the foregoing original form.

In this form, the antecedent proposition being
according to its nature problematic, the consequent
is in a conditional way apodictic: it is necessarily
true if the antecedent, which is in itself only possible,
is true. If we wish to express therewith the truth of
the antecedent, then the assertory form comes into
use: 'Since S is an X, S is a P.' If we wish to
designate that the antecedent is not the condition of
the consequent, the negative form arises: Although
S is an X, still S is not therefore a P.

§ **30.** If now we make prominent the fundamental
thought which the process of thinking has betrayed
through the elaboration of the hypothetical form of
judgment, we discover in it the second fundamental
law of logic: The principle of sufficient reason (*Principium rationis sufficientis*).

The process of thought, as it were, says: You uni-

formly express a necessary truth when you put **S** =
S and **P** = **P**, in an identical judgment. You are
uniformly in error, when you put **S** = **P**, in a categorical judgment; that is, if you suppose it were
ever possible for an **S** to assume for itself alone a
property which does not belong to its concept, or
which it did not have previously; or that, out of a
single principle, a single substance, a single power, a
single thought, it were ever possible for a multiplicity
of substances, developments, or ideas to emerge, —
in general anything manifold out of a unity. It
is, on the contrary, uniformly necessary, if, out of
one subject diverse new existences are to proceed,
that as many conditions differing from one another
should have to be brought to bear upon this subject as there are different results to be derived
from it.

The principle of sufficient reason therefore asserts
negatively (and in this respect is in agreement with
the law of identity) the impossibility of an immediate
connection of the two different contents of the idea,
S and **P** ; *affirmatively*, on the other hand, it asserts
the possibility that, to a combination of two ideas, **S**
and **X**, which somehow determine each other, there
should be given a predicate **P** which is not given
either to the **S** alone, or to the **X** alone. The existing relation between **S** and **X**, whereby this becomes

possible, is the *ratio sufficiens* of the connection of **S** and **P**.

The universal logical meaning of this concept of sufficient 'reason' (*Grund*) consists simply in the supposition, that the manifold content of everything thinkable is not a relationless and dispersed multiplicity; but that there is a *truth*—that is, a sum of such valid relations—through which a definite form of uniting the single elements of the thinkable becomes of itself the equivalent of other elements. In what, on the other hand, those relations consist, in the particular instance or in single large domains of the thinkable; in what, therefore, the definite reason for a definite combination of a certain **S**, or of a certain class of **S**, with a certain **P**, or a certain class of **P**,—is not a matter of logic.

On this account, the principle of the '*ratio sufficiens*' should not be confounded with that of the *causa efficiens*, the law of causation; or with such other general rules as relate to what is actual or to particular classes of what is actual. A 'Cause' (*Ursache*), for instance, is the power that produces something actual, which previously did not exist. A 'reason' (*Grund*) is always simply some valid truth by virtue of which it happens, on the one hand, that a definite effect is attributed to a certain cause; and by which also, on the other hand, in those provinces of thought, in which there is no 'happening,' — for example, in mathematics — the combination of the two contents of the concept depends, in respect to its validity, upon the combination of two others, regardless of time. How this comes to pass, and what is, strictly speaking, involved in the fact, that a condition can be the condition of that which is conditioned by it, — of this no general logical explanation is possible; — with the exception of a single meaning of this question, in which meaning the question is now indeed to be answered.

§ 31. Although we do not ask in Logic to know what consequences follow on what grounds, and by what means the two cohere together, still, if the process of thought is to be able to develop new truths from given ones, we must possess some universal and purely logical principle, independent of our knowledge of the thing to which it has merely to be *applied;* and according to this principle we must be able to judge whether one proposition may be rightly considered as the consequence of another.

Such a principle we do in fact possess. It consists in this, that everything special must conform to its general concept; every individual case to the rule of the general case. Had we not this formal logical principle, then all special knowledge of in-

dividual conditionating relations which actually exist
between any of the elements of existence, would be
of no help to us. We should not be able to apply
them, and deduce any new truth from them.

§ 32. This ‚thought gains expression in the form
of the *general* judgment. Such form is to be distinguished from that of the universal judgment.
The latter, of the form

All S are P,

only asserts that, in fact, all instances of **S** have **P**,
— for example, 'All men are mortal,' — but does
not tell why. Perhaps it may be on account of a
combination of unfortunate accidents which have
no real connection with each other.

The general judgment substitutes the general concept alone for the subject : 'Man is mortal '; or it
indicates by the other form, 'Every man is mortal,'
that the predicate is to be considered valid, not
merely of all actual but also of all thinkable examples of **S** ; and therefore is so by virtue of this
same general concept **S**, and not on other accidental
grounds.

More accurately considered, the general judgment
must besides be included in the hypothetical form.
For it is not the general concept **S** (the universal
man) which is to be considered as **P** (mortal) ;

but every individual, *because* he is man. Therefore, the general form, strictly speaking, is: 'If any **A** whatever is an example of the universal **S**, then such **A** is necessarily **P**.'

§ 33. The form of the general judgment is, nevertheless, still inexact in another way, — namely, in this, that it attributes to the subject the predicate of the general concept, although this subject is not the general concept itself, but only the example subordinated to it ; for instance, the proposition, 'Every material body has some color,' is untrue in so far as the particular body never has color in general, but is either red or green or blue, etc.

That is, the general judgment passes over into the *disjunctive* or *divisive*, of the form, — 'Every **S**, which is an example of the general concept **M**, receives from every general predicate **P** which is attributed to **M**, one of its kinds, **q, r, t,** ..., to the exclusion of all others, as its own predicate. The disjunctive judgment, therefore, furnishes **S** with no definite predicate whatever, but only dictates to it, as it were, the necessary choice between different predicates ; and these, taken together, are individual modifications of a general predicate **P** that is required by the higher concept of the genus **M**, to which **S** is subordinated.

The next step forward would have to consist in concluding this choice and making an actual selection between **q**, **r**, **t**, etc. But this cannot occur, in so far as **S** is a species of **M**, because this reason leaves such choice wholly indeterminate; but must take place on account of the fact that **S** is **S**, — that is to say, because it is such definite species of **M** and none other. For making a decision, therefore, two propositions will be employed; the first of which states what is true of **S**, so far as it is in general *one* species of **M**, the second what is true of **S**, so far as it is *this* species of **M**. These two propositions are obviously the so-called premises of a conclusion, to which new logical form we now pass over. The series of judgments ends herewith, and is not to be extended farther.

REMARK. The ordinary abbreviated form of the disjunctive judgment is as follows:

    a) Affirmative: **S** is either **q** or **r** or **t** or . . .
    b) Negative: **S** is neither **q** nor **r** nor **t** nor . . .

§ **34**. The interpretation of the disjunctive judgment just adduced expresses two laws of thought combined, which have commonly been brought forward as separate formulæ: —

    1. The 'Dictum de omni et nullo'[1] makes promi-

---

[1] On the history of this, compare the *Zeitschrift für Philosophie u. philos. Kritik*, edited by Fichte, Ulrici, and Wirth, vol. lxxvi (Halle, 1880), pp. 48 ff.

nent *positively* the dependence of the particular upon its universal. The expressions which we frequently hear, "What is true of the universal (or of the whole) is also true of the particular (or of the part)," are evidently false. The scholastic formula, "Quidquid de omnibus valet [negatur], valet [negatur] etiam de quibusdam et de singulis," is indeed quite correct; yet it no longer expresses the relation as one of dependence of the particular upon the universal to which it belongs, but only as one of subordination of the unity under the totality with which it is numerically included in the same conception; in this way the proposition becomes, fundamentally considered, a tautology.

2. The second formula, the 'Principium exclusi medii inter duo contradictoria,' is a special case of the more general one which is expressed in the previous section.

That is to say; if we presuppose, in the first place, that the general predicate **P** has three or more species **q, r, t** . . ., and that one subject **S** must, so far as it is a species of **M**, make a choice among these species of **P**, then the choice of one predicate **q** will exclude all the rest, **r, t** . . . ; whereas the negation of **q** does not involve the affirmation of a definite one of the remaining **r, t**, etc. Of these predicates **q, r, t** . . . it is said, that they stand in contrary opposition for an **S**, which is an **M**, to which **M** again **P** belongs.

But furthermore, if **P** (gender) is separable into only two species **q** and **r** (masculine and feminine), then these two predicates stand in 'contradictory opposition' for every **S** which has any necessary relation to **P** (for every living being) ; that is, not only does the affirmation of the one deny the other, but also the negation of the one affirms the other.

Finally, if we wish to avoid the condition, that the **S** have a necessary relation to **P** dependent upon its peculiar nature ; and if we therefore wish to establish two predicates which are contradictory for every **S** whatever ; then such relation can only consist in some **Q** and non-**Q**, — whereby the latter comprehends all that is *not* **Q**. But 'precisely for that reason non-**Q** is not an independent concept, which can be attached as predicate to any **S** whatever ; and, strictly speaking, we no longer have a case of an opposition between two concepts, but of an opposition between two judgments, one of which ascribes a predicate **Q** to **S**, while the other totally denies the same **Q** to it.

C. Immediate Inferences from Judgments.

§ 35. According to an ancient mnemonic coup-let, —　Asserit **A**, negat **E**, verum generaliter ambo,
Asserit **I**, negat **O**, sed particulariter ambo, —

we designate the universal affirmative judgment by
A, the universal negative by **E**, the particular affirmative by **I**, and the particular negative by **O**.   If we
conceive of these four forms as applied to one and
the same content **S–P**, the following relations occur
among them : —

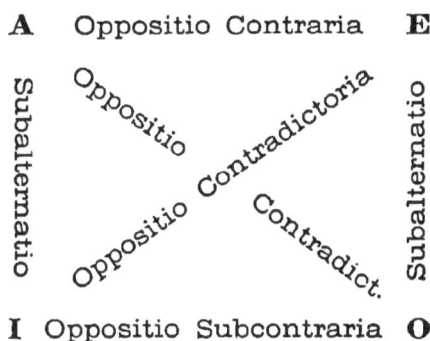

1. Between **A** and **I** (*All* **S** are **P** — *some* **S** are
P), as well as between **E** and **O** (no **S** is **P** — *some* **S**
are *not* **P**) *Subalternatio* — that is, subordination of
the individual to the universal — takes place.   The
validity of the general case always includes that of
the particular instance, the validity of the particular
not that of the general case.   The invalidity of the
general case does *not* carry with it that of the particular ; the invalidity of the particular (which is
always understood as meaning that there is no particular instance whatever in which the content of the
judgment is valid) involves, on the contrary, the

invalidity of the general case. Consequently, we conclude 'ad subalternatam'[1] from $+$**A** to $+$**I**, from $+$**E** to $+$**O**; but *not* from $-$**A** to $-$**I**, *not* from $-$**E** to $-$**O**. Further, we conclude 'ad subalternantem,' from $-$**I** to $-$**A**, from $-$**O** to $-$**E**; but *not* from $+$**I** to $+$**A**, or from $+$**O** to $+$**E**.

Both of these prohibited conclusions — namely, from the particular instance to the general case, and from the invalidity of the general case to the like invalidity of the particular — belong to the most frequently occurring fallacies in logic.

2. From the contrary opposition between **A** and **E** it follows, that the validity of the one excludes that of the other; the invalidity of the one, on the contrary, does *not* involve the validity of the other. We conclude therefore 'ad contrariam' from $+$**A** to $-$**E**, and from $+$**E** to $-$**A**; but *not* from $-$**A** to $+$**E**, or from $-$**E** to $+$**A**.

3. Between **A** and **O** and **E** and **I** there is contradictory opposition. For if **A** is not valid, it is obvious that there necessarily occur some cases, in which the opposite is valid. So then the invalidity of a general judgment involves the validity of the opposite particular judgment; and we conclude 'ad contradictoriam' from $-$**A** to $+$**O**, from $-$**E** to $+$**I**. In the same

---

1 The sign $+$ stands for the validity, and $-$ for the invalidity, of a judgment.

way it is self-evident, that when a *particular* judgment is *not* valid, — that is, when there are no
individual instances in which it is valid, — then its
opposite is universally valid. We therefore likewise
conclude 'ad contradictoriam' from — O to + A,
from — I to + E. Finally, it also is self-evident
that the *validity* of a universal proposition involves
the invalidity of opposite particular ones ; as well as
that the validity of a particular judgment involves
the invalidity of the opposite general judgment.
Therefore we also conclude 'ad contradictoriam'
from + I to — E and conversely, and from + O to
— A and conversely.

4. The subcontrary opposition between I and O,
if one of the two is valid, allows no conclusion to be
drawn. For if one *particular* judgment is correct,
it is possible that the opposite particular is also
valid ; but it is likewise possible that it is *not* valid,
and that the original proposition is only expressed
in particular form but is really universally valid. If,
on the contrary, a particular judgment is denied, then
the opposite general judgment is hereby affirmed 'ad
contradictoriam,' and as a consequence we have 'ad
subalternatam' the validity of the subordinated (of
the previous opposite) particular judgment. We therefore conclude 'ad subcontrariam' from — I to + O
and conversely, but not from + I to — O or conversely.

§ **36.** A judgment undergoes conversion (*conversio*) when subject and predicate are exchanged. The natural interest of thought in this operation consists in this: If a proposition '**S** is **P**' gives to the **S** a predicate, then we may desire to know whether this is an *essential mark of* **S**, whether therefore everywhere, where **P** occurs, the subject with which it occurs is an **S** or a species of **S**. That is, we wish essentially to know whether the converted judgment, '**P** is **S**,' is universally valid, or not.

Pure conversion (*conversio pura*) is the name given to that in which the original and the converted proposition have the same quantity. Impure (*impura* or *per accidens*) conversion is that in which this is not the case.

§ **37.** We may therefore have —

a) A universal affirmative judgment: 'All **S** are **P**.' Three cases are here possible:

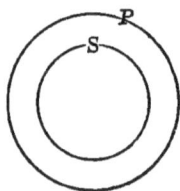
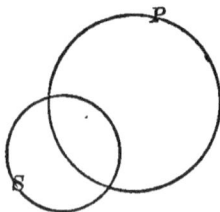
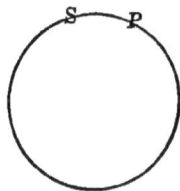

Fig. 1.   Fig. 2.   Fig. 3.

In Fig. 1, **S** is subordinated to **P**: 'All metals are bodies'; in Fig. 2, **S** is subsumed under **P**: 'All gold is yellow.' In both cases it is self-evident that the whole extension of **P** is not covered by **S**; that there are consequently many **P**s which are not **S**; and that, accordingly, the conversion can only be imperfect (*impura*) and give nothing but the particular judgment: 'Some **P** are **S**' ('*Some* bodies are metals,' '*Some* yellow bodies are gold'). — Fig. 3 is therefore to be conceived of in such way, that two equal circles **S** and **P** completely cover each other; from which it follows that the conversion is pure and gives the universal proposition: 'All **P** are **S**.' Such judgments are called 'reciprocable.' But *what* judgments belong to this class cannot be known on logical grounds, but only from knowledge of actual facts. To it, for example, belong all accurate definitions, all correct equations, and many propositions like this: 'All equilateral triangles are equiangular.'

The violation of this rule of conversion is one of the most frequent of logical errors.

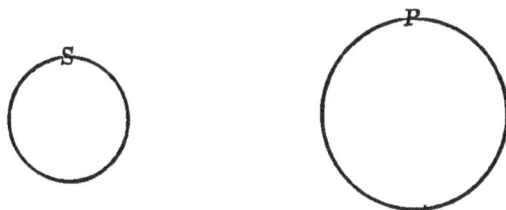

Fig. 4.

b) The universal negative judgment, 'No **S** is **P**,' obviously (Fig. 4) separates **S** and **P** completely, so that it is self-evident that no **P** is an **S** ; that is, universal negative judgments by *pure* conversion give universal negative judgments again.

c) The particular affirmative judgment, 'Some **S** are **P**,' if **S** is subsumed under **P**, — for example, 'Some flowers are yellow' (still more, like the analogous universal judgment, according to Fig. 2) admits only of the particular conversion, 'Some yellow objects are flowers'; if, on the other hand, **P** is subordinated to **S**, ánd **S** is therefore the higher generic notion, — as for instance, 'Some dogs are pugs,' — then conversion gives the universal judgment, 'All **P** are **S**.' This case also we can know only from knowledge of real things.

d) The particular negative judgment, 'Some **S** are not **P**,' can in no rational way whatever be converted into the negative 'Some **P** are not **S**'; for example, from the statement that some monkeys have no tails it does not follow that some things without tails are not monkeys. For the tail might possibly occur only in the case of monkeys, although they might not all have it. Or in more general terms ; the negation of a predicate to any subject does not justify any affirmation as to what of such predicate otherwise occurs or does not occur. All that can be done here is to join the negation to the predicate and convert it into the particular affirmative. Therefore, 'Some **S** are not **P**,' gives 'Some non-**P** are **S**.'

§ **38**. Furthermore, inquiry may be made as to the relations which take place between a subject **S** which has a predicate **P**, and another subject which has not this **P**,— that is, a non-**P**. This leads to what is called *contraposition*. According to this form, the affirmative judgment is changed into a negative, in which at the same time non-**P** is substituted for **P**, the negative attaches its negation to the predicate, and thereby becomes affirmative. Both then become converted according to the customary rules. The 'contraposited' judgment has the opposite quality from the original judgment. The quantity in the particular judgment remains the same; the universal affirmative becomes universal negative, and the universal negative becomes particular affirmative.

Examples :

All **S** are **P**.	No **S** is **P**.
No **S** is non-**P**.	All **S** are non-**P**.
No non-**P** is **S**.	Some non-**P** are **S**.

The conclusions arrived at in this way are not worthless; but they can all be reached more conveniently and clearly without this apparatus of logical formalities.

CHAPTER III.

OF SYLLOGISMS.

A. *The Aristotelian Figures.*

§ **39**. Before we further prosecute the problem
which the disjunctive judgment propounded as that
of the *form of the conclusion,* we have first to allude
to certain other forms of conclusion, which do not
indeed solve this problem, but only express as developed what was already contained in the form of the
general judgment.

In the former case a **P** was attributed to an **S**, in
so far as this **S** falls under the concept **M**. Such a
content is separable into two judgments, one of
which expresses a relation of **M** to **P**, and the other
a relation of **S** to **M**; whereupon the proposition itself asserts as a consequence a relation of **S** and **P**.
These are the elements of the ordinary conclusion :
M is the *medius terminus,* or 'middle concept,' by
means of which a relation is established between **S**
and **P** ; the propositions which express the relation,
in part of **M** to **S**, and in part of **M** to **P**, are the
premises ; the third proposition, which always combines **S** and **P**, and in which **M** does not appear, is

the conclusion (*Conclusio*). According to the different possible combinations of the three concepts in
the premises, the three so-called Aristotelian figures
of the conclusion are distinguished : —

I. Figure:	II. Figure:	III. Figure:
M — P	P — M	M — P
S — M	S — M	M — S
S — P	S — P	S — P

It is only a matter of agreement, and yet one
universally accepted, that in the concluding proposition the concept shall always be the subject which
is combined with M in the second premise ; and the
other one, which stands in the first premise, the
predicate. Accordingly, the first premise may be
in general designated as the 'major' premise (Propositio *major*), the second as the 'minor' premise (Propositio *minor*) ; although, according to the nature of
the thing, no inducement to this is found in the
second and third figures, since their premises are
constructed in a manner quite homogeneous.

For all three figures the universally valid condition
of the cogency of the conclusion consists in the complete identity of the middle term in both premises. For
S and P would obviously not be connected together
through M, if the M with which P is connected were
another M from that with which S is connected.

§ 40. If we consider the position of the premises

in the 'First Figure,' we discover that, according to
the very nature of the case, the same concept **M** can
be at one time subject and at another predicate, only
when it is a generic concept for which the major
premise furnishes a predicate, and under which the
minor premise subordinates some subject as a special
instance or example.

The force of the conclusion, therefore, depends
upon the subsumption of the particular under the universal.   It will, accordingly, take place only when —

1) the major premise is *universal* (for the **S** in
the minor premise, which is an **M**, is with perfect
certainty subsumed under the **M** of the major premise, only in case this latter includes *all* **M**) ; and
when —

2) the minor premise is *affirmative* (for since the
conclusion depends upon subsumption, a negative
minor premise, which would deny any such subsumption, would cut the nerve of the sequence). — On the
contrary —

3) the *quality* of the major premise is not essential
(for the same relation which it expresses between **M**
and **P**, whether it be affirmation or negation, should
and can be carried over in the conclusion to **S** and **P**).
Also —

4) the *quantity* of the minor premise is not essential (for it is just this relation of **M** and **P** that is not

altered by the number of the subjects to which it applies). From this it follows, finally, —

5) that the conclusion always has the quality of the major premise and the quantity of the minor premise (for it borrows from the first the positive or negative relation which it carries over; and from the second, the particular or universal subject to which it carries the relation over).

If the vowels of the following words of three syllables (following the mnemonic couplet of § 35) designate, respectively, the quantity and quality of the propositio major, of the propositio minor, and of the conclusion of the syllogism, then there are four valid so-called 'Modi' of the first figure: Barbăra, Celā-rent, Darii, Ferio.

§ 41. In the Second Figure, the premises establish a relation between two subjects **P** and **S**, and the same predicate **M**.

If now, in the first place, we conceive of both as 'possessing' the **M**, then obviously nothing whatever follows with reference to their reciprocal relation. And the case would be exactly the same as if they both did not have the **M**. Both premises, therefore, should not be affirmative, nor both negative. If, on the other hand, the one subject **A** — particular or universal — either does or does not have the **M**, and the other, **B**, is in the opposite relation with reference to **M**, — not particular but universal, — and therefore uniformly has not or has **M**; then **A** cannot be a species of **B**.

From this it would follow that one premise must be affirmative, the other negative; and that one *must* be universal, and the other *may* be particular as well. Still, since the **A**, which is to be the subject in the conclusion, is always, according to conventional usage, the subject of the minor premise (**S**), the universal premise must be the first or major; and its rules are, accordingly, the following : —

1) The major premise in the second figure is uniformly universal, but its quality is either affirmative or negative.

2) The minor premise is in quality uniformly the opposite of the major premise; but its quantity, on the contrary, may be either universal or particular.

3) The conclusion is uniformly negative, and follows in quantity that of the minor premise.

The four modes (Modi) are : Camestres, Baróco, Cesăre, Festīno.

§ **42**. In the Third Figure, the premises establish a relation between one and the same subject and two predicates.

Now if the subject has both predicates, — that is,

if both predicates are affirmative, — then there follows, from this given example of an actual combination of S and P, the *possibility* of such combination
(the fact that S and P are 'unitable'); and, therefore,
the conclusion is : 'What is S may be P.' This conclusion is customarily (and yet, strictly speaking, not
perfectly correctly) expressed in the particular form :
'Some S are P.' In order that the medius terminus
may both times signify exactly the same thing, and
therefore the M of the one premise may be certainly
contained in the M of the other also, one premise —
it makes no difference which — must be universal.
This gives three modes : Darapti, Datïsi, Disāmis.

If, on the other hand, the M has one predicate, but
not the other, — that is, if one premise is affirmative
and the other negative, — then it follows from this
that the two predicates are separable. Or (to express
the same thing more accurately) the predicate which
occurs is separable from that which does not occur
in this example (that is, is denied). But it does not
follow that the predicate here denied could occur
separate from that affirmed. From

> All animals are living,
> Some animals are not rational,

it does not follow that being rational could occur
without being alive (although the latter could very

well occur without the former). Now, since (§ 39, last paragraph but one) the subject of the conclusion must appear in the minor premise, it must be affirmed ; and, besides, as in the previous figure, in case of two affirmative premises, one must be universal. Strictly speaking, the conclusion merely asserts : 'What S is, P need not be' ; but this again, expressed as a particular judgment (though strictly speaking, not with accuracy) becomes : ' Some S are *not* P.' This gives us the following three modes : Felapton, Ferïson, Bocardo.

Finally, if both premises are negative, then it is customary to assert in treatises on logic that no conclusion is possible — ' ex mere negativis nihil sequitur.' This is absolutely groundless and false. If the same M is neither P nor S, then it follows from this that P and S are not contradictorily opposed to each other ; and that, consequently, what is not S need not, on that account, be P. For example : The just man is not recognized — The just man is not unhappy ; — conclusion : Whoever is not recognized is not on that account unhappy. Conclusions of this kind are by no means to be esteemed as of small value and importance ; since they assert, from affirmative or mixed premises, the unitability or (respectively) the separability of S and P. And they, in fact, are occurring every day, in order to refute some false conclusion which has been drawn from the deficiency of one predicate : " Because thou art not that, thou needest not to be the other also."

§ 43. A Fourth Figure, that of Galen, in which the position of the premises is **P** — **M**, **M** — **S**, and from which the conclusion **S** — **P** should follow, is superfluous and faulty ; for example, —

> All roses are plants.
> All plants need air.
> _____
> Some things needing air are roses.

The *natural* process of thought always draws from the foregoing premises, when it converts them, the following conclusion in accordance with the first figure : 'All **P** are **S** ' — 'All roses need air.' The conclusion of Galen, — ' Some **S** are **P** ' — on the contrary is not merely unnatural, but expresses less than the other. For if it is converted, then we have only the particular proposition : ' Some **P** are **S** ' — ' Some roses are things that need air.' But undoubtedly it is a logical fault, from given premises to conclude less than really follows from them.

And in similar manner, the conclusions possible according to the fourth figure always admit of being obtained more naturally and better by transposition and transformation of the premises in accordance with one of the first three, or Aristotelian figures.

The modes of the fourth figure are as follows :
Bamălip, Calĕmes, Dimătis, Fesāpo, Fresīso.

§ 44. Only the first figure appeared to the older
logic to be evidently conclusive and perfect. The
conclusions drawn according to the other figures, on
the contrary, were considered to be completely justified only when they could be referred ('reduced') by
transformation, conversion, transposition, of the premises, etc., to the first figure ; and then the previous
conclusion drawn from them in accordance with this
figure. The operations necessary for this are signi-
fied by the consonants **s p m c** in the names of the
modes of the second, third, and fourth figures, in
accordance with the couplet, —

> **s** vult simpliciter verti, **p** verti per accid. [accidens],
> **m** vult transponi, **c** per impossibile duci.

That is to say, if m(**metathesis**) requires transposition of the premises (that the major premise be
made the minor premise, the minor premise the
major) ; **s** and **p** call for Conversio (more particularly,
s for pure conversion, simpliciter, **p** for impure, per
accidens) of that proposition behind whose characteristic vowel they stand in the name of the modes.
For example; in order to 'reduce' Disamis to the first
figure, the major premise (on account of the s which
follows its vowel) must undergo *pure* conversion, —

that is, in this case, conversion into a particular proposition ; it is then to have its position exchanged (on
account of the m after the a) with the minor premise. Now from these transformed premises a conclusion is drawn according to the first figure, which
is then in turn converted (on account of the last s) ;
and in that way, finally, the previous conclusion according to Disamis is derived again.

Example :

Original in Disamis :

Some metals are magnetic.
All metals are fusible.

Some things fusible are magnetic.

Reduction to Darii of the first figure :

All metals are fusible.
Some magnetic substances are metals.

Some magnetic substances are fusible.

This conclusion converted :

Some things fusible are magnetic.

Finally, the letter c indicates a more circumstan-
tial operation (the *Ductio per impossibile* s *per contradictoriam propositionem*), which amounts to the same
thing as that, for example, in Bocardo the conclusion
SoP[1] *denies;* accordingly the proposition SaP *affirms*

---

[1] SaP, SiP, SeP SoP, are meant to designate, respectively, a universal
affirmative, particular affirmative, universal negative and particular negative judgment, with the subject S and the predicate P. Corresponding to
these, on the other hand, PaS would be a universal affirmative judgment
with the subject P and the predicate S, etc.

'ad contradictoriam,' and (the c stands in the name
of the modus behind the vowel which designates
the major premise) this contradictory opposite of
the conclusion is put in the place of the major premise of Bocardo. From it as major premise, and
from the second premise of Bocardo as minor premise, a conclusion then follows according to Barbara,
which is the contradictory opposite of the premise
given in fact as the first of Bocardo (and accordingly
is just as certainly false as that is correct); from
all of which it is clear that the negation of the
original conclusion in Bocardo is not permissible,
and that this other is therefore correct.

§ 45. The distinguishing peculiarities of the three
Aristotelian figures are therefore the following:

1) Only the second figure can draw a conclusion
from a negative minor premise; only the third
figure from a particular major premise.

2) Only the first figure can lead to a universal
affirmative conclusion. Only it has concluding
propositions of every kind: **A, E, I, O**; on the
contrary, the second is only negative: **E, O**; the
third is only particular: **I, O**.

This law holds good in the case of connected
series of syllogisms (syllogismi concatenati, catenae
syllogismorum) which originate from the fact that

the conclusion of one syllogism — which is then called 'prosyllogismus' — is employed as a premise for another, which then receives the name of 'episyllogismus.' If the conclusion of the last episyllogism, and therefore of the entire chain of reasoning, is to be universal affirmative, then the entire chain must be constructed according to the mode Barbara of the first figure. If a particular proposition at any place enters into it, then the final conclusion can be only particular; and only negative, as soon as a negative conclusion has anywhere entered into it.

Finally, 'Sorites' (*Kettenschluss*) is the name for certain chains of conclusions that are abbreviated and simplified in expression (abbreviated and simplified by suppressing the concluding propositions of all the prosyllogisms). It is customary to distinguish the sorites of Aristotle and the sorites of Goclenius.[1] The structure and difference of the two are as follows:

Sorites of Aristotle.	Sorites of Goclenius.
$S - M(a)$	$M(z) - P$
$M(a) - M(b)$	$M(y) - M(z)$
$M(b) - M(c)$	$M(x) - M(y)$
$\vdots \quad \vdots$	$\vdots \quad \vdots$
$M(x) - M(y)$	$M(b) - M(c)$
$M(y) - M(z)$	$M(a) - M(b)$
$M(z) - P$	$S - M(a)$
$S - P$	$S - P$

[1] So called from Rudolph Goclenius (1547-1628), professor in Marburg,

§ **46.** Strictly speaking, all syllogisms simply carry over unchanged (as their form of expression makes perfectly clear in case we conceive of those which follow the other figures as 'reduced' to the first figure, § **44**) that relation which the major premise states as between **P** and **M**, and apply it to the subject **S**, which the minor premise somehow obviously includes in the conception of **M**. Accordingly, the nature of the judgment which forms the major premise, as well as of that which forms the minor premise, is unimportant for the form of the conclusion.

If the premises, therefore, are not *categorical* judgments (as we have hitherto exclusively assumed them to be), but if they are furnished to us in *hypothetical* or *disjunctive* form, then these differences (which are, of course, important for the judgments as such) require consideration; but they do not require any alteration of the rules for drawing conclusions which are primarily established for categorical premises. Nevertheless, in some sorts of conclusions with hypothetical or disjunctive premises, the matter-of-fact interest has led to certain artificial expressions to which allusion may be made.

---

author of the 'Lexicon philosophicum,' Francof. 1613, who in his 'Isagoge in Organum Aristotelis,' Francof. 1598, was the first to require for the sorites this (in the series of the traditional syllogistic-norms, comp. supra, p. 57) transformation of the schema of the schools, which is, of course, perfectly correct.

In the first place, there is a series of cases in which a hypothetical major premise, as a general rule, attaches a sequence **F** in the following proposition to a reason **G** that forms the content of its preceding proposition; but a categorical minor premise either affirms or denies the validity either of **G** or of **F**.

a) Now if the major premise asserts positively: 'If **G** is true, then **F** also is always true'; and the minor premise just as positively: 'In all or some cases of **S**, **G** is true'; then the conclusion is: 'In all or some cases of **S**, **F** is also true.' This is called the 'Modus ponendo ponens,' because by positing the reason the consequent is established; and it corresponds to the modes Barbara and Darii.

b) If the major premise were the same, and the minor premise, on the other hand, negative and also assertory: '**F** does not exist'; then the conclusion would be: 'Consequently, **G** also does not exist.' This is a 'modus tollendo tollens' that, by abolishing the result, abolishes the reason which it would have necessarily established in case it had been valid; as for the rest, it is in appearance a type of Camestres and Baroco.

c) If the major premise were negative: 'In case **G** is true, **F** is never true'; and the minor premise asserted positively: 'Now, however, **F** is true; then the conclusion would be: Therefore **G** is not true, which would make **F** impossible, if it were,' etc. This is a 'Modus ponendo tollens' (corresponding to Cesare and Festino), which by positing a result denies the reason which would have made it impossible.

And so forth: — we see that these consequences admit of being referred without difficulty to the course of thought in the Aristotelian figures.

Finally, 'Dilemma,' 'Trilemma' . . . 'Polylemma,' are the names given to those conclusions with a disjunctive major premise (having two, three . . . or many members, respectively) and with several minor premises, whose number is the same as the number of the disjoined members in the major premise ; and which assert conjointly for each of these members one and the same result **T**, or one and the same predicate **T**. The name 'dilemma' (and corresponding to it, trilemma, etc.) is by preference originally given to a conclusion of the form :

If **Z** is to be true, either **U** or **W** must be true,
Now neither **U** nor **W** is true,

Therefore **Z** is not true.

§ **47**. The Aristotelian figures admit of being apprehended in yet another way. If we conclude according to the first figure in Darii :

> All men are mortal,
> Caius is a man,
> ___
> Therefore Caius is mortal; —

it is indeed the *design* of the conclusion to deduce the truth of the final proposition as something in itself still questionable, from the truth of premises regarded as already established. But our attention is soon called to the fact, that '*all*' men are mortal only in case Caius is, too; and that Caius also is a 'man' only in case he has all the essential properties of a man, and consequently that of being mortal. That is to say, the conclusion suffers from a so-called 'double circle': major as well as minor premise, in order themselves to be valid, presuppose the validity of the conclusion which they ought to demonstrate.

Such a mode of drawing conclusions, therefore, cannot be of direct service for the expansion of our knowledge, but only for the purpose of bringing truths already established into a relation of subordination that corresponds to the actual way things go.

1) It can expand knowledge only in case we are warranted in asserting universal judgments, in order to have independent major premises, before the validity of every special instance subordinated to them is proved; — and in case we —

2) are warranted in subordinating a subject to a general concept on account of *certain* marks, in order

to have independent minor premises, before we know whether it has *all* of its predicates.

§ **48**. Now the major premises can be constructed in the second figure, if we expand them somewhat. Its premises are formed quite alike : **P** — **M**, **S** — **M**. In experience it often happens that several of them : **Q** — **M**, **R** — **M**, **T** — **M** . . . are given. But from the premises given just as many conclusions must be drawn as follow from them.

If, therefore, the premises **P** — **M**, **S** — **M**, **Q** — **M**, **R** — **M** . . . are given, — that is to say, if many otherwise different subjects have the same predicate, — then we conclude that not every single one of them has **M** through some special accident, but that one and the same common reason makes it necessary for them all at the same time.

This reason is put forward in the form of a generic concept, of which all the aforesaid subjects are species ; and now the assertion is made that the **M** belongs to this concept **Σ** as a rule, and that those subjects possess the **M** only by means of their subordination under **Σ**. The concluding proposition therefore is : ' Every **Σ** is **M**,' — and this is the simple conclusion of *Induction*, which has its position in the system of thought at this place.

'Perfect' and 'imperfect' induction are distinguished. The first takes place if it is known that
the subjects enumerated in the premises, taken
together, exhaust all the species of Σ. But then,
although the universal proposition, — 'All Σ are M,'
— taken strictly, can be asserted, since the same has
already been asserted in the premises of every single
species of Σ, yet, on the other hand, this concluding
proposition is a bare summing-up, and not a real
expansion of our previous knowledge. For its
change into a general judgment — 'Every Σ is M' —
is not, fundamentally considered, permissible; since
from the mere fact that all species of Σ have one
predicate, it neither follows that they have it as
species of Σ, nor that all species of Σ which are
perhaps still to be discovered will have it.

This last conclusion, if it is made, is nothing more
than the 'imperfect' induction, which concludes from
the fact, that *some* species of Σ have a predicate,
to the appearance of the same predicate in all
species; and which does this, indeed, in consequence
of its common generic concept. But such induction,
although not strictly conclusive as a consequence ad
subalternantem, does expand our knowledge; in
applied logic, however, it requires certain rules to
restrict it.

§ **49.** In a similar way, the third figure can lead to the formation of the minor premises required above. If its premises that have a like construction are increased, — **M** − **S**, **M** − **P**, **M** − **Q**, **M** − **R** . . ., they present the frequently recurring case of manifold properties being attached to the same subject. Here also the conclusion is drawn that each one is not present through some special accident, but that all come from one and the same reason, — and this on account of the fact that **M** is a species of the genus **Σ**, in which the combination of the marks **S P Q R** . . . is prescribed. The conclusion therefore is : ' **M** is a **Σ**,' — which is the simplest form of *conclusion by Analogy.*

This, too, would be ' perfect ' only in case it could be shown that **S P Q R** . . . are, taken together, the entire collection of predicates which **Σ** requires. For, of course, whatever has *all* the properties of a **Σ**, appears itself necessarily to be a **Σ**. And yet this consequence also is not quite strictly drawn. In reality, we can only sum up the premises, and say in the concluding proposition, that in fact all the predicates are found in **M** which belong to a **Σ**. That they are so, however, not merely *in fact*, but by virtue of the truth that **M** is a **Σ**, is never in perfect strictness a matter of demonstration ; but such a conclusion stands on an equality with the so-called 'imperfect analogy,' which draws a conclusion from certain observed marks in M to the assumption that M will also have the other marks which, together with the foregoing, make out a Σ; and that M will therefore *be* a Σ.

B. *The Forms of Calculation.*

§ 50. The doctrine of judgment concluded with the disjunctive form, which asserted that the one or the other special modification of the general predicate P must belong to the S, — which predicate belongs to the higher generic concept of S, namely, to the M. In order that this choice may be decided, it was necessary that S be taken into consideration, not merely as a species of M in general, but also with reference to its specific nature, by which it is distinguished from other species of M.

The first Aristotelian figure, which depends upon this relation of subsumption, does not do this. In the minor premise it only subordinates the S in general, as a species of M; and can, therefore, also only ascribe to it, in the conclusion, the universal P without closer definition. This result is, in part, not correct, since the P in such indefiniteness cannot be a predicate of S; and, in part, it does not satisfy our necessities. For in real life it is seldom enough to conclude : 'All metals are fusible' — 'iron is a metal'

— 'therefore iron is fusible'; but we wish to know how iron *as iron*, in distinction, for example, from lead as lead (that is, perhaps, at what degree of temperature), is fusible.

§ 51. Still another consideration leads to the same demand. Fixed and changeable (historical) predicates of a subject may be distinguished. The manner of drawing conclusions hitherto described referred only to the former. For such properties as belong to a subject by virtue of its subordination under its higher genus, of course belong to it always and are *fixed* predicates.

But in real life constantly, and very often in science, we are far more interested in the *changeable* predicates; that is to say, in those which designate some affection, some activity, some state, in brief, something or other which happens to the S only so far as certain conditions act on S, but which would never flow from the mere fact that S is a species of M (only so much is self-evident, however, that subordination of S under M must establish such a predicate).

This necessity, too, which occurs — for example — in the calculation of all future events, and in the employment of means for our conduct, requires that we should discover for S some quite definite predicate which does not originate from the subsumption of S under a general concept, but from one way of regarding the special nature of the S and of all the conditions acting upon it.

§ 52. The conclusion of *analogy*, too, in case it is to be of any use, requires that, from certain marks which we observe in a subject, we should draw a conclusion directly to the presence of other marks also ; and then from the sum of these marks form a conclusion *secundo loco* to the fact that the subject is one species of a genus. The previous mode of procedure was the reverse of this : in the first place, a subject was subsumed as a species of a genus, and then *secundo loco* a conclusion drawn from this to its predicate.

The question now arises whether that which such analogy could not strictly accomplish admits of being thus strictly accomplished at all ; that is to say, whether we can draw a conclusion from the presence of certain marks or conditions in a subject S, *directly* and without taking our way around through any general generic concept, to the necessary presence or absence, and to the definite value of other marks of the S.

§ **53**. The foregoing necessities would be satisfied by any mode of conclusion, the major premise of which breaks up a general concept, **M**, into the collective number of its parts; and substitutes for it, as holding equally valid, the developed combination of these parts; such a form, therefore, is

$$\mathbf{M} = a + bx + cx^2 + \cdots,$$

in which all the mathematical signs are supposed merely to represent the variety of the possible ways of combining the marks. The minor premise would assert of **S**, not merely that it is a species of **M** in general, but that it is *the* definite species of **M** which we get in case we let some further determining condition act upon the universal **M**. This gives to the minor premise (designated again by a mathematical symbol) the form, —

$$\mathbf{S} = \phi\,(\mathbf{M}).$$

And now the concluding proposition has to express with complete definiteness what predicate must belong to **S**; because the combination of marks substituted for **M** in the major premise has, in the conclusion, experienced the special influence of the conditions designated by ϕ in the minor premise.

One needs no reminder to comprehend that this way of drawing a conclusion is *directly* and *strictly* applicable only in mathematics. In the case of other objects of thought, — for example, concepts of nat-

ural species and genera, — we cannot carry out the
substitution in the major premise ; because we never
perféctly know all the marks of any genus, and still
less accurately all its modes of combination. Further : we can never perfectly show in the minor premise by what determination, ϕ, the genus M passes
over into the species S. If we should be satisfied,
however, with making prominent some single mark
(as x) by which S is distinguished from other species of M (without positively learning from x the
entire nature of S), then we should not be able in
the conclusion to demonstrate what transforming
influence this x must exercise upon all, or upon any
one, of the marks qualitatively different from it (to
which allusion is made in the major premise) or
upon the combination of such marks.

All this is possible only in the domain of mathematics. Since every magnitude is comparable with
the rest, and all are resolvable into the same units,
and producible from them by different combinations ;
and, finally, since they are perfectly defined in their
content, — that is, in their value, and since there
are rules of calculation which determine accurately
the 'Facit' that results in case a definite operation
is applied to a definite combination of magnitudes ;
it is, therefore, possible in this domain actually to
carry out the concluding proposition, and to fill out

in it the schema ϕ (M) by assigning it a definite
value. For example:

$$M = a + b$$
$$S = M^2$$
$$\overline{S = a^2 + 2\,ab + b^2.}$$

This limitation to mathematics, nevertheless, does
not rob such a conclusion of its place in Logic.
For calculation, too, is a process of thought, — and
that not the most unimportant. On the other hand,
it is to be considered that we succeed in an absolutely certain expansion of knowledge only in so
far as we can refer the objects of our reflection to
relations of magnitude, and can make calculations
with them.

§ 54. But if such an application of calculation to
concepts of qualitatively different content is to take
place, and if we are to be able to conclude from the
existence and value of one mark to the existence
and value of another, then the connection of the
two and the dependence of one on the other, although it does not admit of being placed upon a
strictly logical basis, must be presupposed as a matter of fact; and nothing further can be done than by
calculating according to a general law which holds
good for such a condition of dependency, to assign
to every given value of the one mark the value of

the other belonging to it. This is done in the form
of a proportion:

$$e : \mathbf{E} = t : \mathbf{T}.$$

The proportion does not refer the content of the
one mark back to the qualitatively different content of the other mark, but allows both to be what
they are. It also makes, in general, no comparison
whatever between the absolute magnitudes of the
changes which the two correspondingly experience.
For these two, — since they are measured by quite
different standards, — are frequently not comparable.
Strictly speaking, it only compares the number of
the units of change which both marks undergo (the
change in each one as measured according to its
own standard), and from the given number for the
one mark determines the corresponding number for
the other.

It is self-evident that almost all application of
mathematics to real objects depends upon this manner of drawing conclusions; further, that proportions are possible *exactly* only where the marks of
the real object are determinable quantitatively; but
that they run into inexact comparisons with reference to other objects of thought.

§ 55. The above-mentioned expression for a proportion contains one further inaccuracy. If **E** be

the expansion and **T** the temperature, then the aforesaid expression leads to the idea that there are two
marks which, absolutely and without reference to
the subject in which they occur, stand in an unalterable relation to each other. But *how much* the expansion increases for every additional degree of
temperature, depends on the nature of the body
heated, and is different in the case of different
bodies. Indeed, the necessity that one mark should
exercise any influence on the other depends simply
on the fact that they are marks of one and the same
subject. This is true for every pair of marks. And
we are on this account obliged to apprehend the
nature of the subject as a *law* such that from it
flow the proportions of all its single pairs of marks.

Mathematics, and that in Analytical Geometry,
has, indeed, approximately discovered a formal expression for this logical demand in the comparison,
for example, of the different curves, in which it
defines the entire nature of a curved line, its shape
and its direction, etc., by means of a proportion
between the corresponding increments of the ab-
scissas and ordinates.

Such comparison also depends, of course, on the
fact that all the properties which can belong to a
spatial figure — for example, its curvature and the
like — after all depend simply upon different mag-

nitudes of the *same* species; and no qualitatively incomparable properties occur. An extension of this logical form to the treatment of real objects — for example, the attempt to discover a formula for the nature of man similar to that which we possess for the nature of the ellipse — is a problem of infinite complexity and quite impracticable with any exactness. But approximately the attempt has always been made to solve it, since there has been an effort to discover a so-called 'constitutive concept' for every object.

That is to say : — a merely '*distinguishing*' concept, such as barely suffices to render its object distinct from other objects but does not positively and exhaustively tell in what it consists, is held to be different from a '*descriptive*' concept, which as far as possible specifies completely the content of its object, but makes no essential distinction in order of rank between marks that are more original and 'law-giving' (as it were) and such as are derived and dependent. Finally, there are distinguished those '*constitutive*' or '*speculative*' concepts (or the ' Ideas') which are limited to designating a certain primitive content (*Ur-Inhalt*) of the object, from which all its individual marks and their combinations are then derived as its necessary consequences.

C. *The Systematic Forms.*

§ **56**. For the discovery of such a 'constitutive'
concept,' we remind ourselves — as we have already
done in the doctrine of the concept, — of the fact,
that the isolated consideration of an object in itself
does not teach us how to distinguish the essential
and 'law-giving' marks in it from the unessential
and dependent. That in it which gives it its law
we find in the 'universal' which is common to it with
others of its species. By this means we are con-
ducted to the path of *Classification;* and we suppose
that we know the 'essence' of an object just as soon
as we are able to assign to it its position in a 'System,' which begins with some most general concept,
subordinates to this many general concepts as species, — and finally, to the latter a variety of particular concepts.

§ **57**. It is not quite this problem, but a more
superficial one, which is fulfilled by the so-called
'artificial classification'; such as either develops all
its species or single instances from one general concept **M**, or one general case **M**, — or else subordinates these particulars to **M** as though they were
already well recognized. The following operations
are distinguished :

1) The Partition of **M** into its different marks, $a, b, c \ldots$

2) The Disjunction of each of these marks into its species; of a into $a_1 a_2 \ldots$, of b into $\beta_1 \beta_2 \ldots$ etc.

3) The Combination of every single species of each predicate with every species of every other predicate; hence $a_1\beta_1\gamma_1, a_1\beta_1\gamma_2 \ldots, a_1\beta_2\gamma_1 \ldots,$ $a_2\beta_1\gamma_1 \ldots$

4) The Arrangement of the species of **M** thus deduced, either according to well-known lexical principles, or according to some other that answers the ends of use.

5) A Correction by which the non-valid or impossible species are again removed; — species which, accordingly, originated from the fact that we have had regard only to the presence and not to the mode of the combination of the marks $a \ b \ c$ in **M**. It is possible that some modifications of these marks, — for instance, $a_3\beta_2\gamma_2$, — do not admit of being combined in this way at all (example : **M** = triangle, a = angle, b = side, a_1 = right, a_2 = obtuse, angle, β_1 = equal, β_2 = unequal, sides. Hence $a_1\beta_1$ is impossible).

This whole mode of procedure is seldom used for deducing its species from a concept **M**; for the most part, the species are previously known, and are only arranged under the **M**. Much oftener it is of service

in developing, from a general case **M** (some judgment), the special instances conceivable; and, here,
just that which excites our interest is to know, which
of them are possible or impossible, and what standard
— for instance — is of real use, what absurd.

§ **58**. Artificial classifications, strictly speaking,
systematize the way which we must take for a survey
of the content, rather than this content itself. The
single species stand side by side, excluding each
other, — without any knowledge of their nature origi-
nating from such knowledge of their arrangement.
This particular problem of classification, — to wit,
the determining of the 'essence' of each species by
its position in the system, — accordingly leads to the
fresh attempt to arrange the species of a concept **M**
in the so-called 'natural classification,' in a single
series or in series of series, in such manner that
they form a steady advance from the most imperfect
to the most perfect.

That two species may more or less adequately correspond to their general concept, the marks of which
they must both possess collectively, is possible on
account of the fact that the marks combine in very
different magnitudes, and the relations between them
may be thought of in a variety of special forms and
different degrees of strictness. For example; from

general logical pre-judgments, that species is held to be perfect which has all the marks uniformly elaborated; and that to be imperfect in which some marks disappear and others occur in excess. But such pre-judgment constantly needs correction or supplementing from a knowledge of the real thing; and only in the particular case does it admit of being determined from this knowledge of the thing, whether the aforesaid uniformity, rather than a definite inequality of the marks, agrees more adequately with the *meaning* of the universal.

But in order to be able to speak of any such 'meaning,' it is further presupposed that the general concept M is itself also a member of a higher series, and has its position in this series side by side with N, O, P, . . . as other species of a yet higher universal; so that, by virtue of this position, a definite problem is proposed to it, according to which it may be estimated, which of its own species is the more perfect, since it best answers this problem.

And so the series of these presuppositions proceeds. For a place in a series that is still higher, and, finally, in the comprehensive series of the entire coherent system of the universe, must be discovered for the series M N O P, — a place which it assumes, and from which some light is thrown upon the direction of that forward movement from the lower to the

higher which goes on in itself. Without such a complete demonstration as matter of fact for the basis
of these valuations, all natural classifications, which
are limited to a single domain of objects, events, or
even concepts, remain incapable of logical proof.
Since they only lay at the foundation some general
concept, the direction of whose development they
suppose to be known, they are productive of assertions that, although suggestive and not untrue, are
not so *exclusively* true as would be demanded in such
a case as this, where that 'constitutive concept' is
required for every single concept, from which its
entire mode of behavior shall be deducible.

§ **59.** Besides these avoidable deficiencies, the natural classification has yet one other that is universal
and unavoidable. The 'constitutive concept,' for
which we are in search, ought above all to explain to
us, how its content must behave, react, or alter, in
case certain conditions act upon it. Of all this, classification teaches us nothing whatever. It simply
furnishes an *indication* of the 'meaning' which the
content of the concept — thought of as unchangeable
— has in the series of species, in connection with
which it expresses the nature of a general concept.
But it does not explain how it can originate, exist,
maintain itself, alter, or perish.

It may be left undecided, which of two logical forms satisfies a higher necessity. Certain it is that the aforesaid 'indication' alone is not enough ; that it absolutely cannot be substituted in the place of 'explanation' ; and, finally, that the latter belongs to those problems of life which are practically most urgent.

§ 60. *Explanatory* science, which undertakes the latter problem, is distinguished from classification, by its form, as follows :

It does not, like the latter, take its point of departure from a single concept ; and it does not develop its conceivable species as though it were self-evident that all which such concept postulates for its complete manifestation is, on this account alone, also possible or already actual. But rather since, as concerns this latter point, — and as concerns the manner in which the content of the concept behaves under any given conditions, — it is of course, not the concept alone, but only some rule which holds good for it and likewise for such external condition that can decide ; explanatory science begins with one or more judgments which are propounded as *general laws*. They are therefore of such a kind that both their subject and their predicate (or their major premise and their minor premise) are universal and comprise under

them many particular instances; but it is the content of the judgment which determines the rule, according to which one of the instances of the minor
premise depends on one of the instances of the major
premise.

Now since nothing results from general laws in
themselves, the second necessary element is a series
of *facts*, expressed either singly or collectively, which
themselves then take the place of general cases, and
by which in each single case that definite modification
of the content contained in the major premise or in
the subject of the general law is designated, in
reference to which a determination of its minor premise or its consequent is sought.

Now new knowledge originates from the subordination of the fact under the law, on account of the
fact needing to be known only partially, — perhaps
on *one* of its sides, — in order to be capable of subsumption under the law; but, in consequence of such
subsumption, some one of its sides, previously not
recognized, becomes defined and recognized. The
most essential problem of explanatory theory, nevertheless, does not consist in this simple sequence of
the conclusion, but in demonstrating the reciprocal
influence which very many conditions, that are independent of each other, exercise upon each other in
case they act on one and the same subject; and in

setting forth the entire nature of the subject as the collective resultant of the complete circle of its conditions (comp. the 'Applied Logic').

§ 61. The spirit of explanatory theory is at variance with that of classifications.

The latter think not merely to *explain* the individual by the general concept, as a species of which they apprehend it, or by its position in the series of other species; but also to *legitimate* it. That is to say, only by means of the fact that it is a species of a general concept which has its well-known place in the total order of the world, does a *justifiable existence*, as it were, belong to the individual. It would be untrue or obscure, if we could not answer the question, — What is it? — by pointing out its general notion.

Explanatory science surrenders the thought abovementioned. It attaches no value, for example, to the statement whether any particular object lying before us is a 'plant' or an 'animal.' It bids us investigate, out of what elements, in what proportion and form of combination, the object consists; and what forces, according to what laws, are active between these elements, and between them and the outside world. If we are certain of this, then we know the whole object and its whole present and future mode of behavior. But the answer to the question, whether it is an 'animal' or a 'plant,' adds nothing whatever to such knowledge. Complete cognition consists therefore in this; — in apprehending every object as the final resultant which proceeds from the action and reaction of different conditions or forces; which forces not only act collectively for laying the basis of this individual object, but also everywhere else act according to general laws, and only produced *this* object because they found themselves in *this* rather than in some other one of many forms of combination possible to them.

§ 62. It is evident that explanatory science does not furnish perfect satisfaction to our desires for knowledge. It treats every phenomenon, every event, only as an unimportant example of general laws, and as a result of many conditions co-operative in fact, but which it was not necessary should co-operate at all, or in precisely such a manner. The objects are, accordingly, deprived, by the very manner of considering them, as well of their inner unity as of the necessary character of their existence. It can only be said hypothetically that, in case such or such conditions prevail, then the object must be so or otherwise. But it remains undecided what conditions actually do prevail.

Against the foregoing mode of apprehending the
truth, the fundamental thought of classification certainly presents a just consideration. It is necessary
to suppose that not merely do general laws hold good
in the world, while the arrangement of the facts on
account of which a definite form of actuality flows
from the laws is, on the contrary, given over to
chance, uncontrolled by any principle; but rather
that in the arrangement of the aforesaid facts also,
a principle (that is to say, an 'Idea') is effective, and
that this principle fixes beforehand the whole arrangement of the final result, the whole system of
the future phenomena which are to be actualized by
means of the aforesaid facts in conformity to the
laws.

The *Ideal of Cognition* would therefore consist in
finding for the 'Things' such 'constitutive concepts'
or 'Ideas' as not only determine their meaning and
significance, but also show how this meaning itself
reaches its own actualization, by bringing together
the necessary conditions and forces. This problem
leads us wholly beyond the limits of Logic, and can
only be taken up again in so-called *real* Philosophy
(comp. the 'Encyclopædia of Philosophy').

Second Principal Division.

Applied Logic.

SECOND PRINCIPAL DIVISION.

—◆—

APPLIED LOGIC.

—◆—

CHAPTER I.

APPLICATION OF THE FORMS OF THE CONCEPT.

§ **63.** All communication of an inner state, whether it be feeling or thought, is an attempt so to direct the inner activities peculiar to another as that this other must himself have a vital experience of the very content which is to be communicated. No content can ever be carried over *ready-made*, as it were, from one mind to another.

Now, much admits of being communicated only by physically transposing the other person into the state in which he must experience the matter in question. We turn him toward the light or strike him, in order that he may know what 'brightness' or 'suffering' is. In other cases, as in art, we produce a mental mood, since we indirectly, by means of a series of changing ideas, conduct the mind through a series of individual feelings.

Thoughts, on the contrary, are assumed to be capable of a logical communication, which consists in this, that an accurately defined series of combinations and separations of individual ideas, supposed to be well known, is prescribed to the other person; and then exactly the conception which is to be communicated remains with him as their logical resultant. There are two opposite methods of doing this: the explanation of a concept by *abstraction*, and its explanation by *construction*.

§ 64. We explain by 'abstraction' in case we abstract from single examples of the concept to be explained that are better known to us than is the concept itself, everything which is so special as not to belong to it; so that it alone remains for us to contemplate. Necessarily, however, this occurs only in the case of all such simple concepts as, for example, 'Being,' 'Becoming,' 'Unity,' etc., whose content does not consist of a conjunction of other ideas.

The second way, that of 'construction,' which endeavors to build up the concept from its constituent parts, must, at least, be attempted in the case of all composite concepts. For 'abstraction' makes the content of the concept intuitable only as a whole; but teaches us nothing concerning its interior structure. 'Construction' is perfectly practicable only in affairs of mathematics; because here the meaning of the individual ideas which are to be combined, and of the forms in which they are to be combined, can be fixed unequivocally. In the case of other concepts, which combine marks qualitatively different in manifold relations, neither of these things is possible. And on this account, wherever it is possible, the intuitive image is included in the explanation.

Now, Definition is that kind of construction which endeavors to build a concept up by means of merely logical operations. Fundamentally considered, it uniformly regards the greatest part of the work as already achieved since it itself refers to some higher general concept which is known, and which already contains that entire mode of combining all the marks which is so difficult of elucidation. To this, definition adds a specific mark, which suffices to distinguish the concept in question from other species of the same universal; but it entrusts to the imagination, along with this, the task of conceiving the other corresponding specific marks, which here take the place of what is universal in the general concept, and in connection with it form the entire nature of the thing to be defined. Nevertheless, where the attempt is made to enumerate them all, the definition becomes a *description* which, on account of its

imperfectibility, is not valid as a proper logical
form.

§ **65**. It is essential for definition that the concept of genus applied by it should be the one *next*
higher — the 'Genus proximum.'

Definitions that are too wide, and adapted not
merely to what is to be defined, but also to something else which we wish to distinguish from it, arise
in case we choose instead of this *genus proximum*,
some far higher general notion as our point of departure ; for in that case the 'Nota specifica' does not
always admit of being included in such a way that
nothing else, too, falls under this definition. This
mistake is frequently met with in the practical
domain, in that it is customary to use a very high
and pre-eminent general concept for better recommending some proposition.

Too narrow definitions adduce marks that are not
necessary to what is to be defined, and therefore
exclude some of its kinds. They easily originate
from the limited nature of our circle of experience,
which accustoms us to only a few of the more nearly
allied species of the universal.

Definition perpetrates a '*Circle*,' in case it assumes
in the explanation that which is to be explained,
although under another form. This mistake always

originates, in case we aim to define constructively simple concepts — like 'Being,' 'Becoming,' and others similar — which are to be made clear only by means of abstraction.

Finally, the custom of apprehending substantively all things that are to be defined, even when they are by nature verbal or adjective, although not itself a mistake, is one inducement to mistakes. It is more natural and conformable to our purposes to define thus: "A body is elastic, in case it, etc."; or, "An organism is alive (or is diseased), in case it, etc.," than to define thus: "Elasticity is" . . . or, "Life (disease) is, etc." The latter modes of expression are indeed often quite harmless; but they are also often productive of the habit of treating states, properties, and events as though they were substantial and independent beings.

§ 66. The task of definition, which is not merely to specify the content of the concept, but also to limit it with respect to other concepts, can often be accomplished only by arbitrarily fixing the usage of speech.

In the first place, there are certain concepts which have no secure point of departure for their validity, like the collective ones, 'throng,' 'heap,' 'bald-headed'; then there are others contradictory to each other, between which a point of indifference exists, such as 'cold' and 'warm,' and the like. In all the former cases a limit is wanting, at which the concept begins to be valid ; in the latter, the limit is also wanting at which they pass over into the contradictory concept. We do not know where 'warm' ceases and 'cold' begins ; we only know in what direction of the series the cold diminishes and the warmth increases, and the reverse.

Another great multitude of concepts has originated in the living formation of speech, in such manner that, when comparing what is particular, we, at one and the same time hold to several points of view that are independent of each other. Accordingly, those species which fall under the concept attained, agreeably to all these points of view at once, indubitably belong there ; on the contrary, other species, although they appear to fall under it as judged in one respect, in other respects, on the other hand, appear to be excluded from it. In such a case nothing remains to be done but to fix, for the exact use of science, the extent of the concept, and accordingly the significance of its name, in a way that agrees with our purpose but is somewhat arbitrary ; and not to take too much pains simply to remain in accord with the usage of speech. The concept of 'disease,' for example, comprehends, on the one hand, every deviation from the normal condition; on the other, it signifies a condition which has a variable course; in the third place, it signifies such an one as is fraught with danger. Just so the conception of 'crime' has respect, simultaneously, to the bad will, to the execution of the deed, to the magnitude of the harm done, etc.

§ 67. With reference to the value which we ascribe to the fixed limitation of concepts as set over against each other, our ordinary process of thought controls, sometimes by means of a principle of logical pedantry, and sometimes by means of one of logical frivolity.

The former holds every distinction in concepts insurmountable (the well-known mode of speaking: "that is something quite different"); the other regards every distinction as fluid, and teaches how to change every concept by intermediate stages into any other that is in any degree allied to it. This change is accomplished by altering at pleasure the magnitude of individual marks, — many (such as are necessary to the new general concept, but wanting in the given concept) being considered as present but of no value, and others (such as are present but do not belong to the new general concept) being regarded as such that they must be inserted in these examples also, and that they are wont to occur only in certain of its kinds without being of any value.

All these logical transformations have their correct
use in art, where they are the servants of wit ; and in
ordinary life they are most frequently employed in
excuses, in cases where the intent is to deceive concerning the real worth of some action by means of
approximating its content, piecemeal, as it were, as
much as possible toward something innocent. Even
in science they are of the greatest value in the right
place. But proof is always to be demanded that in
the nature of the realities with whose concepts we
are dealing, there lies the possibility or the actual
custom and the effort, of making such transitions.

§ **68**. Of every object a variety of concepts is possible, since it can be subordinated to each of its own
marks and to every possible combination of them.
Among these concepts one may be preferred, —
namely, that *constitutive* concept, which we previously
sought for, but found only approximately and in a
few domains, such as in the concepts of species belonging to the creations of nature.

Nevertheless, the interests of our thinking seldom
require this concept ; and every process of investigation is accustomed only to consider certain single
sides of an object from which it deduces consequences in accordance with general laws. Accordingly, it is for the most part only a prolixity, and

often a source of inaccuracy as well, when we forcibly aim to have an exhaustive speculative conception for an object which we are treating ; and then, when after all we cannot for the most part attain it, pursue an inaccurate approximation thereto. It is more useful to take our point of departure from 'partial definition,' which unites into one general concept only the properties important for the shifting investigation; and then, of course, modifies the consequences that flow from the subordination of the object under *this* general concept, by having regard to the other peculiarities of the object. Thus, for example, medicine has to bring 'man' under the concept of a mechanism consisting of physical elements ; while national economy has to bring him under the concept of capital to be produced. But both must limit the consequences drawn therefrom by the reflection, that this 'mechanism' and this 'capital' possesses likewise reason and will.

One of the principal sources of sophistry will be such partial definitions, in cases where we draw consequences from them but neglect to introduce into them the modifications which are requisite on account of the rest of the nature of the object, although this is not included in the definition. Little as this mode of procedure is scientifically permissible, yet its application is justified in poetry and rhetoric.

CHAPTER II.

§ **69**. In a judgment, what interests us practically is its truth. Now the simpler case is this, that a proposition with a definite content is given and its proof is required; the more difficult case is this, that the discovery of a proposition still unknown is demanded.

All adducing of proof — to which we now turn our attention — must begin with the demonstration of the validity in fact of the given proposition. That is to say, if it is discovered by means of a test which is made of it either by experience or by single examples, that it has no such validity whatever, then all pains taken with adducing proof is wasted. This rule is not always sufficiently observed, and numberless prolixities arise in science as well as in ordinary life from the attempt to explain facts — that is, to demonstrate them as necessary — which have no existence at all.

Only after the validity of the proposition is established, does the adducing of proof for its justification begin, — that is, the demonstration that it has a *right* to be held valid as a consequence of other truths and facts.

§ 70. The fact needs no explanation, that all adducing of proof whatever presupposes a number of propositions which are not, in their turn, in need of proof, and which are also not capable of such proof.

These propositions are ordinarily comprehended under the name of *axioms*. Fundamentally considered, they fall into two classes: the one comprehends 'assertory judgments' which express certain actual facts, and which, taken collectively, are derived from experience and admit only of the above-mentioned proof of their validity. The other comprehends the just as undemonstrable 'principles of reason and consequent,' in accordance with which alone, from any fact or truth a conclusion can be drawn to some other. The latter, strictly speaking, are hypothetical general judgments, which do not tell what *is*, but merely what *must* be if something else is.

A criterion for affirming that any proposition is an axiom of the latter kind lies only in the unconditioned nature of the evidence with which it announces itself in consciousness as necessarily valid. Nevertheless, since erroneous prejudgments also can, from a variety of reasons, unlawfully attain in our mind such evidence, it is necessary to test the truth of any proposition in question, not merely on its own evidence but also on that of the impossibility of its contradictory opposite. If the latter is not demonstrable, then

the axiomatic and unconditional validity of the proposition in question does not stand beyond doubt.

§ **71.** Proofs are distinguished, in accordance with
their proximate aim, as *direct*, which demonstrate
the given proposition immediately, and *indirect* ('apagogic'), which primarily demonstrate the impossibility of its opposite. Only the first kind are able to
specify, in explanatory fashion, the grounds in right
for the truth of the proposition; the second always
prove only its validity in fact. In convincing force,
however, the first is not always unqualifiedly to be
ranked as superior to the second.

The direct, as well as the apagogic, proof is uniformly either 'a principio ad principiatum,' from reasons to consequents (progressive, forward-moving);
or else it proceeds 'a principiato ad principium,' from
consequents to reasons (regressive, backward-moving).

The different forms of proof that spring out of the
foregoing fact have a very different value;—partly
in general, and partly different according to the domains of the content to which they are applied.

§ **72.** The 'direct' proof can be *progressively* (and
therefore in such a manner that the process of thinking takes the same course, from reasons to consequents, as the nature of the thing) carried on in two
forms.

1) The proposition in question is considered as the terminal point of a conclusion ; we therefore take our start from truths that are more general and already established, and from them, by subordinating other general or special sub-propositions, deduce the required thesis as a necessary conclusion. This form is of all most to be preferred ; because it contains, or may contain, the complete exposition of the thesis.

2) The thesis may be regarded as a point of starting, and since it is considered valid, its consequences developed. If these are at variance neither with general truths nor with established facts, then the validity of the thesis is — not indeed certain, but probable. For since all the consequences can never be developed, it remains possible that, in case we were to proceed yet further, some contradiction would still be revealed. As proof of the truth, accordingly, this form is not perfectly stringent. On the other hand, it occurs in practical life, for recommending certain proposals, as a proof of their conformity to an end.

Regressively also, ascending from consequents to reasons, the direct proof may run its course in two forms. That is to say —

1) The thesis in question serves as a point of starting, and is, therefore, here regarded as a consequent from which we ascend to its reasons. Now if the reasons

which must hold good, in case the thesis is to hold good, are in thorough accord with general truths, then primarily only the conceivability or possibility of the thesis is demonstrated thereby; and only in domains where (as in mathematics) all that is conceivable has *eo ipso* the truth which appears in the particular case, does such proof include the truth of the thesis. In relation to everything actual, accessory proof would be necessary, to the effect that the causes are in existence which must actualize the thesis, as yet in itself only possible. In practical life, on the other hand, this form of proof is perfectly sufficient — for example — to found or defend a legitimate claim. Finally —

2) The thesis can in turn be regarded as the terminal point; and therefore in this case as a reason. We then take our start from certain other propositions or facts that are known to be valid, and show that the sole ground of their possibility is to be found in the validity of the thesis, which thereby is made necessary. This proof is therefore conclusive, but is difficult to adduce; and it often stands in need of accessory proofs, in order to show that the thesis is not merely an adequate reason for the aforesaid facts, but is the exclusively possible and sole reason for them.

§ 73. 'Indirect' proof cannot, strictly speaking, immediately demonstrate that the opposite of the given thesis — that is, the antithesis — is not valid in fact ; or, in more general terms, the refutation of a proposition can never be the *immediate* conclusion of a proof. For never do anything but merely positive — that is to say — valid consequences (such as, for the rest, can consist in affirmative and negative judgments) follow from all such principles as could be chosen for grounds of proof ; and only on account of the fact that these consequences exclude the antithesis, is the latter explained as not valid.

The *first progressive* form, which sets out from general truths and shows the antithesis to be impossible, accordingly cannot occur. What appears as this, is invariably a *direct* progressive proof, which exhibits the necessity of some proposition by which the antithesis is excluded.

On the contrary, the *second progressive* form, that proceeds from the antithesis, which is assumed as true, to its consequences, and the *first regressive*, that proceeds from the same to its presuppositions, are both of great value as apagogic proofs ('Deductiones ad absurdum '). They demonstrate the invalid nature of the assumed proposition by showing that, either the consequences which would flow from it, or the reasons which must validate it if it is to be valid, are not compatible with general truths or existing facts. Now although they do not contain the grounds for the validity of the thesis whose antithesis they demonstrate to be impossible, still they are often to be preferred to the tedious and involved direct proofs, on account of the pictorial way in which they show the absurdity of every proposition contradictory of the thesis.

The *second regressive* form would draw a conclusion from facts to the impossibility of explaining them by the antithesis as their ground; and this obviously is practicable only in case the necessary properties of such a ground are first positively defined, and it is then shown that the antithesis is thereby excluded.

§ **74.** Besides the distinctions already alluded to, a further one is made which has to do with whether a universal proposition (for example, one concerning the triangle) is directly proved in its universality, or in such manner that the demonstration first applies to all individual instances (first for the right-angled triangle, then for the acute-angled, and finally for the obtuse-angled) and then the proofs are summarized. Such collective proof requires that we should be in a condition to enumerate all possible individual instances which the general case *can* contain; and even when this is done, it always has the disadvantage of simply establishing the validity in fact of the proposition demonstrated for all examples of the universal; but it neither proves nor explains how this validity follows from the proper nature of the universal. Although it is often quite indispensable, since the nature of a concept or of some general case is often not so widely known, that we should be able to recognize the grounds which it contains for the universal validity of some assertion concerning it.

Related to the foregoing is the *proof by exclusion*. This form, likewise, in case of a complete disjunction, enumerates all the conceivable individual instances of a general case, and proves of all the rest, except one, that they are impossible; so that in case it is established at all that some one species of the universal must occur, then this one left remaining is necessarily valid.

Finally, the limitation of a given value between two limits — for example, the proof that a is neither greater nor less than b, and accordingly equals b — belongs in this connection.

§ 75. In all the forms of proof alluded to, we have assumed that the conclusion follows as to the whole, according to the first figure, — that is, by subsumption of one proposition under others. We speak of the proofs by analogy and induction further on.

This being presupposéd, the question may arise, how proofs are discovered, — by which we mean, the superior propositions on which the validity of the proposition in question depends; as well as how the inferior propositions or auxiliary constructions are divined by whose mediation the latter flow from the former.

On the whole, Logic cannot teach how to 'discover' such proof; but it can only admonish us that in every science stereotyped methods of proof for the single groups of related problems are developed, which put every one, who understands how to bring a problem under its own group, upon the right way. Besides this only one indication is possible, — namely, that the ground for the truth of a proposition, which expresses not merely a fact, but some mode of procedure that is dependent on other truths, must invariably be contained in the content of the proposition itself, when the latter is perfectly thought out. Synthetic judgments cannot be given in such a way as to add to the subject **S** a predicate **P**, which is neither contained, nor has its ground, in the complete concept of **S**. Such a predicate would be false. All correct judgments are as respects their content, *analytic;* or rather they are 'identical' and merely appear synthetic in form, since one and the same content can be designated in both subject and predicate, from points of view that are very different and arbitrarily chosen. Accordingly, in order to find the proof on which the correctness of a proposition is founded, one must analyze subject and predicate and the combination between the two, and add all the latent accessory thoughts which are meant thereby; in this way one will see in this complete content of the proposition, for the most part, its own proof of itself.

It frequently proves of advantage to consider as not yet valid the subject of the thesis, or the premise to which this is attached as a consequent; and to let it originate from another subject or another premise whose predicate or conclusion has already been established. In this way it is more easily shown how, by the changes of this other subject into the one in question, the predicate in question also originates from this other. If the different instances of a universal proposition constitute a series, — as often happens in mathematics, — this proof takes the form of a 'proof from n to $(n + 1)$'; in such manner that the given thesis is first verified for some special case or value of n, and then it is shown that, in the formation of each next case $(n + 1)$ from the case n, the conditions, by virtue

of which the proposition of n holds good either are
maintained unchanged or are reproduced, or else
equivalent conditions take their place.

§ **76.** The *Fallacies* in proof, which logic, alas!
can only mention and not teach us to shun, are the
following :

'Petitio principii,' or 'the circle in proof' (Diallele)
is committed, in case what is only some other expression for it, or some consequence of the conclusion
which is first to be demonstrated, is employed as an
argument.

'Fallacia falsi medii' (Quaternio terminorum) consists in the fallacy of taking, in one of the conclusions
that constitute the proof, the medius terminus in
both premises, in a different signification. The
inducement to this is not far to seek in the case
of abstract conceptions, whose signification has
equivocal elements ; and also in the case of such
empirical concepts (to which allusion has already
been made) as are likewise formed by abstraction
in accordance with different points of view.

In this connection the 'Fallacia de dicto simpliciter ad dictum secundum quid' may be referred to ;
that is to say, the fallacy of applying a proposition,
which in itself holds true universally and absolutely,
to definite circumstances, without limiting and modi-

fying it in such a manner as these circumstances require. This fallacy is in ordinary life the princi- ple of Doctrinairism and unpractical Idealism, — of 'riding principles horseback.' Conversely, the 'Fal- lacia de dicto secundum quid ad dictum simpliciter' extends a principle, valid in a single instance, to all instances, — even to such as are lacking in those conditions that give grounds to or recommend its validity. In practical life this is the principle of pedantry and 'philistrosity.'

'Nimium probare,' and therefore 'nihil probare,' is the fallacy of demonstrating the validity of a proposition, not merely for the subjects and cases for which it holds good, but also for others for which it does not in fact hold good, or should not hold good. The fallacy comes from the choice of a false argument, or from an otherwise correct argument not being limited to those of its sub-species which alone perfectly contain the ground for the validity of the proposition. 'Parum probare' is in itself only a fallacy of method, because that which is proved is correct. It becomes a logical fallacy only when the validity of the proposition which is demonstrated for a number of cases, is at the same time appre- hended as a negation of its validity in the other cases, in which it in fact also holds good.

'Hysteron-proteron' (ὕστερον πρότερον), in distinction from petitio principii, is the awkwardness in method which from two propositions **A** and **B**, that may be in turn deduced from each other, makes that one the ground of the proof which would be more fitly exhibited as the result of the other.

Finally, 'Heterozetesis' (ἑτέρου ζήτησις), or 'Ignoratio elenchi,' is the complete aberration of the proof, — arriving at a conclusion which was not to be demonstrated at all.

§ **77.** Finally, we distinguish 'Paralogisms' ('erroneous conclusions') as undesigned fallacies in proof, from 'Sophisms' ('fraudulent conclusions'), — that is to say, thoughts *designedly* so combined that from them, in a way formally correct, either something wholly absurd and false originates, or contradictory assertions flow from them with equal correctness. The first case, again, always depends upon designedly committing some one of the customary fallacies in argument. The others, the so-called 'Dilemmas' that were specially celebrated under that title in antiquity (the 'liar,' the 'crocodile,' etc., — comp. § **46** at the end) originate in this way; the content of a judgment **A**, which taken logically by itself must be either correct or incorrect (without any regard to the circumstances under which it is ut-

tered, or to facts not as yet established) is nevertheless apprehended as though it were conditioned
in its meaning or in its validity, by just those circumstances ('the liar') or by these not yet established facts ('the crocodile').

CHAPTER III.

§ **78.** The second problem, to which allusion was previously made (§ **69**), — namely, to discover some general proposition — divides again into several, the first of which is the discovery of a universal judgment, that comprises a number of particular facts. This may take place either in such manner that the same content which a single fact expresses is demonstrated as valid in general for all instances of its recurrence; or in such manner that a more general proposition is sought for, which embraces within itself as classes all the given facts.

§ **79.** The first case only furnishes us the occasion to observe that the assertions — " Experience teaches nothing universal "; and " What is correct in one case need not be so in another," — are not rightly made. Quite the contrary, it follows from the law of Identity, that a truth which is valid once cannot fail to be valid a second time; accordingly, that every individual experience is once for all valid, — that is to say, the same predicate is again valid at all times for all cases of the recurrence of the same subject.

The difficult thing is simply to determine *in praxi* whether a second instance does actually repeat precisely the subject observed in the first case. For this the probabilities are different in different domains of research. For example, it is enough for the chemist, if he once knows that he has some element before him in a *pure* state, to observe its reaction toward some other element a single time, in order to establish it forever. The zoölogist, on the contrary, will hold some peculiarity of a new animal, only one example of which has been discovered, to be 'normal,' that is, to be valid in general (since disease and malformation are possible in such a case), only when the analogies of other classes of animals justify him in this assumption.

§ 80. The second problem would be to deduce a general judgment of the form — "All S are M" — from individual perceptions, which (as previously alluded to) bear the form: P is M, Q is M, R is M, etc. This is the *simple conclusion by imperfect Induction*, to which allusion was previously made.

It was shown in the Pure Logic that this inductive conclusion serves for the widening of our knowledge only in case it is imperfect, — that is to say, it follows, without strict conclusive force, from the fact that some kinds of S have the predicate M, that all kinds of S possess it. The precautionary rules, which would be required to make the conclusion at least as probable as possible, are simply as follows.

With the rising number of cases in which M occurs among the species of S, the probability that it belongs to all S increases of itself. Nevertheless, every circle of human experience is limited, and we can at least never be *sure* from that which we learn to know only by experience, whether we are not merely getting a view of certain particular species, nearly allied, which do indeed all possess the predicate M, and yet do not possess it by virtue of their general concept, but on account of their other concordant special marks. For this reason it is necessary to show that the M, which we wish to ascribe as universal to the concept S, occurs not merely in the case of very manifold and very diverse species of the S, but also occurs specifically in the case of such *pairs* of them as are related to each other, with reference to some mark which can be depended on for having some influence on the establishment of M, in the most contrary fashion possible. It can then be concluded that the reason for M, or for the subject to which M belongs, can only be some generic concept like S, which is common to all the species.

§ 81. This same problem is much more important for us in another form. That is to say, it is only rarely of much use to us to show that a **P** is united with a general generic concept **S**, and belongs to all species of **S**. As a rule, we desire still further to know on what *ground* **P** belongs to **S**. This, expressed in general form, leads to the problem of searching for the conditions on which the occurrence of an event depends in all the otherwise diverse instances of its repetition.

In experience we almost uniformly meet with a complex of diverse facts, $a + b + c + \cdots = U$, with which another just as composite complex, $a + \beta + \gamma + \cdots = W$, stands in combination. The problem is to ascertain whether in general **U** is the condition of **W**, and what particular part of **U** forms the condition of what particular part of **W**.

The means for such investigation are, either the facts which observation yields spontaneously, or likewise such others as we add by experimentation.

Observation, for the most part, shows us effects which depend on a large number of conditions at the same time; many of which, moreover, are wholly withdrawn from observation. The main end of experiment does not consist simply in multiplying facts, but in permitting only a fixed and accurately known number of conditions to be in every trial. Experiment further consists in separating these conditions, whenever it is possible, so that in every trial only *one* is active, and yields an unmixed result, or, at least, so that in every trial only a small number of conditions co-operate, and, accordingly, the part of each single condition in the collective result admits of being determined by comparison of the different trials, in the way of elimination. Finally (a matter concerning which we shall speak later), experiment especially seeks to secure the *measureableness* of the magnitudes of the conditions and of the results.

§ **82**. The following general cases serve simply as examples of investigation :

1) If **W** (the effect) uniformly follows upon **U** (the cause), then it is possible that the reason for **W** lies in **U** ; and it remains a matter for inquiry whether the *whole* of **U** furnishes the reason for **W**, and whether some other condition besides **U**, that is uniformly connected with it but unobserved, is not necessary in addition. But it is just as possible that **U** and **W** are *co*-effects of a common cause, **Z** ; and also possible, finally, that **U** and **W** occur together by a merely fictitious coincidence, without any causal connection whatever.

2) After **U** has occurred, **W** is sometimes wanting. Then **U** either is *not* the cause of **W**, or **U** and **W**

are *co*-effects of $(Z \pm Y)$; so that **W** occurs if **Y** is positive, and not if it is negative; or **U** is certainly the adequate, and perhaps the only reason which can produce **W**; but there is in the cases that occur some hindrance which prevents **U** from producing its uniform result.

3) Suppose that **W** occurs before, or without, **U**. Then there is either no connection between the two, or the two are again co-effects of $(Z \pm Y)$; or, finally, **U** is not the *only*, although the quite sufficient, reason for **W**, but there are other equivalent reasons.

4) Suppose that **U** falls out or is experimentally removed, and then **W** does not follow. In this case it is either a mere coincidence, without real connection (which is, however, extremely improbable, and is only to be assumed in observation, and not in experimental treatment); or **U** is, or contains, the condition of **W** (which is most probable); or, finally, **U** and **W** are *co*-effects of **Z**, and the same interference which hindered **Z** from producing **U**, hinders also the production of **W**.

5) If **U** vanishes or is removed (experimentally), but **W** remains, then there is either no nexus between them, or they are again *co*-effects of **Z**; but this time in such manner that the interference with **Z**, which hinders **U**, permits **W** to exist; or else **U** is

the cause of the origin of **W**, although not the cause of its continuance.

The proposition " Cessante causa cessat effectus " is false in this general form (indeed, if it were not so, all our labor and action in the world would be illusory). In general only those effects vanish with the vanishing of the cause, which the cause would further have had in case it had not vanished. Effects already produced, on the contrary, continue after the cessation of the cause, in so far as they consist in states of things which are not in contradiction with the proper nature of things and with the external conditions in which they stand. Only in the opposite case would they need a maintaining cause; and this is then, besides, not always the same as the producing cause.

6) Further, in case the part **a** disappears from **U** = (**a** + **b** + **c**) and **W** is not altered, then one condition of the continuance of **W** does not lie in **a**, although perhaps the condition of its origin may. Consequently, we have to investigate, where it is possible, whether **b** + **c** alone produces **W**; in which case **a** would be a superfluous part of **U**.

On the other hand, if the whole of **W** disappears with the vanishing of **a**, then **a** alone may be the sufficing condition of **W**. Such condition, however, may just as well lie in the entire sum (**a** + **b** + **c**), so that **W** always vanishes whatever part of **U** is removed, but does not depend on any one of them alone. This is often overlooked ; — for example, when some one part of the brain, **a**, after the destruction of which a function **W** ceases, is physiologically considered as the sole organ of **W**.

7) If two different complexes of causes — **U** = (**a** + **b** + **c**) and **V** = (**m** + **n** + **c**) — produce the same effect **W**, then **W** will for the most part undoubtedly depend on the **c** common to both. Still it is possible that **c** is quite without any direct significance ; and that, on the contrary, (**a** + **b**) and (**m** + **n**) furnish two equivalent pairs of causes, in which one and the same condition for **W** is only differently distributed to the single elements.

8) Finally : if again (compare what is said under 6) **U** = (**a** + **b** + **c**), and **W** also vanishes with the removal of **a**, then **a** may be the sole cause of **W** ; but it is also possible that such cause lies only in **c**, but **b** is a hindrance to the efficiency of **c**, which was, on its side, balanced by **a**.

The foregoing possibilities might be indefinitely multiplied.

§ **83**. Now tne ascertainment of the fact that any particular **a** is the condition of some *a* or other, does not give us satisfying knowledge, as long as we are

unable to subsume under such a proposition certain
others, not wholly like it but only of similar kind; —
that is to say, as long as we do not know according
to what general law *a* is changed by a fixed difference,
in case **a** is also changed by another fixed difference.

Now since determinations of number merely, and
not marks of quality, are deducible from each other
in thought according to general laws, the problem is
as follows ; — to seek for the law according to which
the values of the magnitude of the results depend
upon the magnitudes of the conditions belonging to
them.   This is a problem which must be solved for
the most part experimentally.

§ **84.** If it is found that, when the magnitude of the
condition remains uniformly the same, or increases
uniformly or diminishes uniformly, the results dependent on it do not alter their values in a perfectly
parallel way ; but — for example — when the value of
a increases, that of **a** for some time increases, and
then while **a** keeps on always increasing, assumes a
diminishing value : then this is a proof that **a** alone
does not contain the complete reason of **a**, but that
still other conditions co-operate ; and that these either
consist in accessory conditions which are independent of **a**, or in alterations which the object affected
by **a** experiences through the earlier influence of **a**,

and which oppose resistance, sometimes uniformly and sometimes periodically, to the further influence of a.

In all such cases as the foregoing, there is a demand for a further preliminary investigation. For although we can often discover very simple general laws for the course of such a composite effect, — as, for example, the laws of Kepler show; yet after all we can only grasp perfectly the whole of it, in case it can be demonstrated as the resultant of a combination of single effects, whose laws are such that a constant increase in the result belonging to *it* always corresponds to the constant increase of each single condition. The place of such a preliminary investigation is in part supplied by a further employment of the previous artifices, and in part by *hypotheses*.

§ 85. If we have discovered experimentally a series of corresponding values for the conditions and the results, then the intricate nature of the thing sometimes compels us (for example, in many problems of statistics), inasmuch as many conditions that are changing independently of each other always co-operate, to confine ourselves to the collection in tabular form of the appropriate material.

On the contrary, where it is possible to make the transition to a general law which expresses the dependence of every member in the series of results upon the corresponding member in the series of conditions, this transition always remains a kind of logical *saltus*. For no measuring, since it all invariably depends upon nothing but the sharpness of our perception by the senses, gives us absolutely accurate numbers. Accordingly, if the series of values discovered for the results accords accurately with that calculated by a general formula from the values of the conditions, it is only extremely probable but not certain that such formula is the correct law. If it does not agree with them, but must be corrected in order to agree, then it is possible that another correction would make it explicable with equal facility by another law. Nevertheless, if perfect certainty is wanting, still a probability, which is to be estimated as quite equal to it, may be attained for the correctness of a law. This is principally done by measuring the discovered series of values according to different standards of measurement, and arranging the experiments so that the dependence of the results on the conditions is subject to observation from different points of view. If the same formula fits in all such altered expressions of the thing, then it will be the correct one.

§ **86**. On this account, the discovery of a general law is frequently called an 'Hypothesis.'

We employ this word in a more limited meaning.
Hypotheses are conjectures by which we endeavor
to divine something real that is *not* given in perception, but of which we make the supposition that it
must be existent in actuality, in order that what *is*
given in perception may be possible ; — that is, may
be comprehensible in the light of those laws of the
connection of 'Things' which are recognized as
supreme.

Among the rules, by following which we endeavor
to give the greatest possible certainty to hypotheses,
it is incorrect to lay down the general one, that *simplicity* is a criterion of truth.   We must rather distinguish the nature of the cases.   If we have to do
with establishing by hypothesis a relation which is
very general and which unites almost all that is
actual, then 'simplicity' is most probably the correct
thing.   On the other hand, to explain a fact which
manifestly depends on very many co-operating conditions, a very simple hypothesis about it only awak-
ens the suspicion that all the difficulties of the matter
are not observed, and therefore not explained.

As for the rest, no rules can be given which assist
the intelligent process of discovery in the formation
of hypotheses, but only certain ones which limit it.

It is of use in the first place, to make it perfectly
obvious, what are the demands which some matter of

reality, when hypothetically assumed, must necessarily fulfil, in order to satisfy the phenomenon that is to be explained. This admits of being established with a perfect cogency by concluding backwards from the phenomenon itself. From these abstract but unquestionable parts of the hypothesis, a further special elaboration of it is to be distinguished, which endeavors to divine the concrete matter of fact in which the aforesaid demands are found to be actually fulfilled. Very often several such matters of fact are possible. The hypothesis should not blindly choose the one which first falls in our way ; but it must previously survey the entire domain of related phenomena, in order to ascertain what kind of matter of fact is *wont* to occur therein.

Now if a hypothesis has been framed with this reference to a rather large number of related phenomena, then it very often happens that the progress of experience contains new facts, for whose explanation the previous hypothesis does not suffice. It must, accordingly, be altered by new additions. This 'building of hypothesis on hypothesis' is not to be avoided in the course of our scientific labors ; and, on this account, it is incorrect to forbid it. Only it is certain that the investigation is not to be regarded as ended until these hypotheses, composed piecemeal, at last admit of being gathered together again into one simple assumption corresponding to the simplicity of the thing itself.

Finally, the rule — "not to frame any hypothesis whose content lies beyond the borders of a possible counter-proof" — is indeed an excellent one ; but in many domains of investigation, exactly where we are most in need of hypotheses, it is not practicable.

§ 87. Hypotheses are conjectures by means of which we suppose that we are divining an actual matter of fact. *Fictions* are assumptions which we make with the consciousness of their incorrectness.

We are compelled to resort to fictions, when — for example, in practical life — judgment must be passed upon a case which does not exactly fall under any single known rule ; we are then compelled to indicate it in such a way that it can be subsumed under that rule which is recognized as over some content most nearly related to its own.

We are further compelled to adopt fictions, when in science there are no modes of experience which admit of a *direct* application to the data of some problem before us. In this way, for example, curved lines are regarded as interrupted straight lines (which they never are), and reckoned accordingly.

In both cases it is, of course, necessary to correct the consequences which flow from the general ground of judgment assumed by the fiction, with reference to the fact, that the case in hand is not exactly subordinated thereto. And on this supposition, fictions lead — for example, in mathematics — back again to exact results and not merely to approximations.

Finally, fictions are very frequently, besides, employed as means of illustration, with the purpose of bringing intricate relations, that obviously, as frequent perception shows, belong to some case **a**, to apply to a case **b** which possesses relations that, although not wholly the same, are essentially similar.

§ **88**. Fictions of themselves lead to the procedure called '*Analogy*,' which, although it does not propose to extend a proposition to a subject that is certainly not to be subsumed under it, still does transfer a proposition from one subject to another, on account of the similarity of the two.

This procedure depends upon the perfectly cogent principle, that what is like must under like conditions assume like predicates, and under unlike conditions unlike predicates ; just as what is unlike must under like conditions assume unlike predicates.

But the first half of this proposition avails nothing for the extension of our knowledge ; and the other only slightly, because it yields no positive result, but only teaches us that the predicates are *not* like.

Accordingly, such principles, strictly speaking, are productive only in mathematics, where it is possible to determine the *degree* of the unlikeness of the subjects and that of the conditions, and consequently also to reduce the unlikeness of the predicates to a definite measure, and to give them a positive content.

Outside of mathematics, the principle that what is similar assumes similar predicates under like conditions, although always correct *in abstracto*, is still a very difficult one to apply; and after all, everything comes to this, that we gather from it what group of marks $(x+y)$ is present in **A** as a cause of the predicate **P** being attributed to the **A**. For if **P** is to be transferred from **A** to some **B**, on account of the similarity of the two subjects, then **B** must be like or similar to **A** in relation to $(x+y)$; — that is to say, must have this group of marks in common with **A**; in which case, on the contrary, all other similarity of **A** and **B** is of no avail whatever.

Now that $(x+y)$ *is* the condition of **P** can be demonstrated partially on other grounds; and, in case **P** is ascribed to the subject **B**, is no longer a conclusion from analogy, but a *direct* sequence. If such proof can *not* be adduced, then different subjects must be compared as far as possible : and it must be shown that all their other similarities cannot produce the common predicate **P**, unless

($x + y$) is a common constituent of all the subjects;
and that, on the other hand, difference of the marks,
otherwise, does not destroy the common character
of **P**, as long as ($x + y$) remains common to all the
subjects. From this, finally, the conclusion is drawn
with a satisfactory degree of probability, that the
predicate **P** will belong to all subjects in which
($x + y$) is found.

§ **89.** The other kind of problem (§ **78**) is this, —
to demonstrate the reality of a single fact.

Three different points of starting may be discovered for this purpose. That is to say, we have before us given facts which we can apprehend either
as causes, or as results, or as accompanying signs
of the fact in question.

In none of these ways is a strict demonstration
possible. For even if what is given always contains
the complete *cause* of what is to be proved, yet this
cause after all — since we are here not dealing with
valid truths, but with actual occurrences — may be
hindered by counter-forces from the production of
its effect. But if what is given can be explained
from what is to be proved, as its *result,* still it is
never demonstrable with such perfect cogency that
other equivalent causes could not also be assigned
for the same given fact. Finally, that the mere

reciprocal companionship of two facts, because it ordinarily occurs, does not establish any certain conclusion from one to the other, is self-evident.

§ 90. The general principles, in pursuance of which we try to give as much of probability as possible to this 'proof from *indiciae*,' depend upon the following general views.

In reality a multitude of different causal nexuses, which do not issue from one principle, constantly run on side by side. Now it is not probable that any one of them will, escaping all disturbance from the others, produce the effect, abstractly belonging to it, in its entirety and without abatement. On this account, finely spun plans, which do not have regard to 'accidents,' appear to us in practical life convicted of folly; and in art and history all representations appear improbable which make an intrigue succeed in *all* its results, or an important factor accomplish *all* its theoretically correct results for hundreds of years together.

But, on the other hand, it is just as improbable that an extraordinarily great multitude of causal nexuses, independent of each other, should have intersected each other in such a manner as to produce exactly one special matter of fact that, in the form in which it exists, is comprehensible from some

single other cause. Accordingly, we do not believe
in the efficiency of a thousand minute causes for the
production — for example, in history — of a result
which flows of itself from some one 'direction of
the Zeitgeist,' so-called. Nor in medicine do we
credit the view, that every symptom of a patient
has its separate harmless cause, as soon as the sum
of all the symptoms exhibit the unity of a 'disease,'
as arising from which they are all comprehensible.
Just so in jurisprudence we do believe in such a
diabolical concatenation of a thousand minutiæ that
from them the appearance of single coherent 'crime'
originated.

§ **91**. The importance of the single indiciæ is
estimated according to the same rules as in cases
of inductive proof ; consequently, the probability of
the instance to be proved is referred back to internal
grounds of actual fact.

Now there are instances enough where the probability of the occurrence of an event cannot be judged
at all from grounds of mere fact ; either because, as
in the case of future events, we do not by any means
know them all, or because it would take us into
details too much to estimate actually even the part of
them that is known. Here, however, it may not be
necessary to have an opinion about the occurrence

or non-occurrence of the event, in order to base upon it some practical procedure. Nothing remains for us in such a case but first to enumerate together, as precisely *alike* possible, all the *possible* instances for the occurrence of which wholly like reasons testify; and then to ascribe to each of them a like probability of its occurrence, or else (in case of problems where we are dealing with a manifold repetition of analogous events) the same frequency of appearance. Its probability is therefore measured by a magnitude which divides the certainty that some one case must occur (which is here put at unity) by the number of all the cases alike possible with it.

This probability is distinguished from that previously discussed, which rested on grounds lying in the very nature of the single case, as one which occurs precisely where no such grounds exist. It is in no respect a theoretical assertion about what will actually occur in the future. For nothing prevents, in spite of the calculation, the one case from always occurring, and all the rest of the equally possible cases, from not occurring. Such probability is rather, in reality, a *practical standard* by which we endeavor to determine the measure of the future confidence that ought still to be cherished in the occurrence of a definite single event among many that are alike possible.

§ **92.** The purely logical interest taken in *choices*, *votes*, etc., does not consist merely in the attaining of some result, but also in this, that each of the single judgments from which it is to be attained (that is, in this case, each *opinion*) should find opportunity for a complete and direct expression. Practical interests, on the contrary, and the considerations which are had besides in both cases, are opposed to this in many ways.

The logical interest is perfectly satisfied only when a choice is direct, — that is, when it relates only to one object of choice, is followed by 'aye' and 'no,' and accordingly makes it possible to give an unmixed expression to the negation. All other choices, which are directed to several objects of choice at the same time, which are followed merely with positive votes, and therefore permit the negation of the one object to be made only by affirmation of some other, are logically deficient. They do indeed furnish a result by means of the majority. But it remains possible that some other result would have satisfied in like manner the collective will of those voting; since, although the result actually reached is somewhat preferable to the majority, it is on the contrary decidedly disagreeable to the minority; while the other result would have been scarcely less agreeable to the majority and the only one agreeable to the minority.

It depends upon the nature of the relation which the choice induces, whether the more *decided* satisfaction of the majority, or one less perfect but more equalized among the entire collection of choices, is to be preferred.

As a purely logical question it is taken for granted that the constituency of voters all vote together on a certain matter (that is, as united into *one* collection), and form only a single decisive majority. On practical grounds, however, they are frequently divided into a multitude of groups to be treated separately, and the establishment of the definite result of the choice follows on the ground of the majorities which appear in the single groups; so that, if the vote for a candidate should be taken by aye and no, he would be chosen as soon as — in case the whole were divided into nine groups — he had for him five of these groups (each one, according to its majority). It can easily be understood that in this way the decision may be reached by a minority of those entitled to vote at all in the matter on hand. If we divide 100 votes into 10 groups of 10 each, or into 20 groups of 5 each; then we have, in the first case, $6 \times 6 = 36$, in the other $11 \times 3 = 33$, as the number of votes necessary for a decision, — instead of 51, which without this partition into groups, in case the 100 voters gave their vote together, would be required for a majority. It can be calculated that, under such circumstances, the number of votes necessary to a decision may perhaps fall as low as a quarter of the whole number. And a still smaller number is sufficient, in case the number of the votes is not placed as equal (as we have done hitherto), but different, in the single groups.

§ 93. In voting on proposals for laws, which seek to satisfy one and the same necessity by formulating it in ways different and exclusive of each other, the usage employed accords, strictly speaking, at only *one* point with the logical interest. That is to say, if the voting assembly wishes not to recognize in principle the general thought which underlies all these ways of formulating it, or the necessity itself; then this cannot be satisfactorily done by successive negations of the single proposals, but only by a 'motion to fix the order of the day,' which must always be established as soon as such a vote of the whole body is expected.

From this point on, however, the logical procedure must either be such that a decision must be reached by an aye-and-no vote upon *every* proposal of the kind, and that one of them all retained which gets the majority of affirmative votes; or else, at least, one of the proposals must first be selected by merely the votes in favor of it, without any further issue, so as to make obvious what is the condition of opinion thereupon.

The actual procedure is frequently much more speculative as to its want of obvious significance, or at least admits the existence of such speculation. For whatever the order of questions may be, yet custom hinders, by the affirmative of any question of all those that follow being excluded from the vote, as well the free expression of opinions as also the attainment of a result that is wholly accommodated to them. For every aye or no has in this case a double significance; either it means a choice (or non-choice) of the individual proposal in itself considered, or an affirmative (or negative) for it from fear (or hope) of defeating (or carrying) by this means some subsequent less (or more) agreeable measure. Accordingly, the procedure passes out of the purely logical domain into that of practical political calculation and trickery.

II.

ENCYCLOPÆDIA OF PHILOSOPHY.

INTRODUCTION.

§ 1. 'Philosophy' should not be considered as an employment of the thinking faculty, which attempts to solve problems of its own, that are otherwise wholly unknown, by means and methods just as peculiar and otherwise unheard of ; and which, therefore, makes its appearance as a kind of luxury superfluous to our real life. The rather is it nothing else than the strenuous effort of the human spirit, by a coherent investigation, to find a solution, that is universally valid and free from contradictions, for those riddles by which our mind is oppressed in life, and about which we are perforce compelled to hold some view or other, in order to be able really to live at all.

Life itself involves, in that which we are wont to call 'education,' numerous attempts at such a solution. As well concerning the nature of things and their connection under law, as concerning the grounds of beauty in phenomena, and, finally, concerning the

rules obligatory for human conduct, education is
accustomed to establish a number of trains of thought
that excite a great interest on account of the liveli-
ness and warmth which they possess as witnesses,
not for unprejudiced reflection but for life's immediate experience. Their disadvantage, however, consists in this, that they are not connected systematically together, are often contradictory of each other,
and are as a rule interrupted before they have attained the ultimate ground of certainty. Aroused
by certain events, which happen to one man in one
way and to another in a different way, all these reflec-
tions retreat in a lively manner some steps backward,
in order to discover the reasons that will explain such
experiences. They then ordinarily come to a halt,
and regard as sufficiently ultimate principles certain
points of view, which themselves include what is yet
more of a riddle. It is natural that many such trains
of thought, setting out as they do from different
points of view, should not coincide in one whole but
leave gaps and contradictions between them.

The same relation maintains itself with the individual sciences. They attach themselves to single
domains of actuality, and are satisfied when they
discover principles which are constantly valid within
such a domain, but which at once become doubtful
in their application on being carried over to any other

domain. Thus the conception of a cause that acts according to law is undoubtedly valid in physics. But the consideration of organic life, as well as ethical speculations, frequently oppose to it the conception of a cause that is determined only by its ends and not by laws, or of one that acts with a complete freedom. It is the problem of philosophy to determine the claims of these different principles and the circuit within which they are valid. Accordingly it admits, for the present, of being defined as the endeavor, by means of an investigation which has for its *object* that which is the *principle* of investigation in education and in the particular sciences, to establish a view of the world that is certain, coherent, and of universal validity.

§ 2. To this entire undertaking two presuppositions are necessary.

The first is this, that there exists in the world at large a 'truth' which affords a sure object for cognition. This assumption has seldom been called in doubt. To its denial there stands opposed, principally, the moral conviction that without such truth the world would be *absurd;* and that the world cannot after all be this.

The other presupposition is, that *we* are in a condition to apprehend this truth, — although by no means necessarily the whole of it; and yet some part which shall serve us as a firm basis for an investigation that is not perfectible in particulars. In opposition to this assumption, doubt arises in three forms :

a) A Scepticism that is without *motif* raises the question whether, at last, all may not be quite different from what we are necessarily compelled to think it. This doubt we pass by. For since it does not arise out of the content of what is necessary to thought, but only demands in a general way some pledge for the truth of our thinking, that lies outside of all our thought, no satisfaction can ever · be given it, but it can only be overcome by a conviction of the absurdity of its own content.

b) A second kind of Scepticism, with a *motif*, endeavors to show that the thoughts which we are compelled to think according to the necessary rules of our cognition are frequently impossible according to rules just as necessary ; and, therefore, that what is a necessity to our thought does not lead us to any true knowledge. Such doubts are not to be refuted or confirmed, without investigation. We derive from them simply the rule of circumspection, accurately to test the most general conceptions and principles which appear to us as necessities of thought ; to separate what they in truth mean and prescribe from the more special and not necessary adjunct thoughts, such as have attached themselves to the former during their application to limited circles of objects; and then to see whether, in this way, the contradictions are made to vanish.

c) As related to scepticism and derived from it, Criticism endeavors to establish cognition more securely, since it premises an investigation of the nature of the faculty of cognition, and thereby seeks to determine the limits of the validity of our forms of cognition, previous to their application to their objects. Nevertheless, although a preliminary orientating of ourselves concerning the origin and connection of our knowledge may guard us against many vain undertakings, yet we cannot regard the undertaking of criticism as anything more than a *petitio principii.* That is to say, previous to the application of knowledge to things, we cannot do anything but become conscious of those grounds of judgment which our reason contributes to the consideration of things as necessities of its thought. Whether these principles are applicable to 'things themselves,' does not .admit of being decided in a preliminary way from the history of the genesis of our cognition; because, in order to have such a history at all, one must necessarily already have taken one's point of departure from actual presuppositions concerning the nature of things cognizable, concerning the nature of the cognizing spirit, and concerning the kind of reciprocal action that takes place between them.

§ 3. We therefore enter upon our philosophizing with the confidence which reason has toward itself,— that is to say, with the principle that all propositions which remain, after the correction of all accidental and changeable errors, as always and universally necessary to thought, are put by us at the foundation of everything as confessedly true ; and that according to them must our views concerning the nature of things be determined, and from them alone must a theory of our cognition be obtained.

But as concerns the *way* which we are to take in our philosophizing, two views are distinguished. Both are at one so far as this, that the world itself must be a unity ; and consequently the perfected cognition of it must be, as it were, a closed system, which can contain no parts that are not united, or that stand toward each other without any ordering whatever.

One view, however, believes that it is both able and obligated to divine at the beginning the One Real Principle, on which the world actually depends, and from it to deduce or construe the entire actuality as the sum of its consequences. Such a beginning for cognition would be the best if we were gods. On the contrary, as finite beings, we do not ourselves stand in the creative centre of the world, but eccentrically in the hurly-burly of its individual sequences. It is not at all probable and is never certain, that we should perfectly divine the one true Principle of the world in any one fundamental thought, however noble and important, to which some sudden intuition might lead us; still more uncertain that we should formally apprehend it so accurately that the series of its true consequences should obviously proceed from it. It is rather altogether probable that the first expression of the principle will be defective, and that mistakes will always multiply in the course of the deduction; since one has regard to no independent point of view from which they might be corrected.

The second view — of which we fully approve — distinguishes the investigation from the exhibition of truth. The mere *search for* the truth is by no means under the necessity of taking its point of departure from one principle, but is justified in setting forth from many points of attachment that lie near each other. It is only bound to the laws of thought, — beyond that, to no so-called 'method' whatever. All direct and indirect means of getting behind the truth must be applied by it in the freest manner possible. The. latter, however, — the exhibition of truths already *gained* — has only to satisfy the need for unity and systematic coherency. But for it, too, this is a problem of which we do not know beforehand in how far it is solvable.

§ 4. A preliminary division of Philosophy may be attempted simply with the design of separating the different groups of the problems, each one of which appears to be self-coherent and to require an investigation of a specific kind. We attribute little value to the reciprocal arrangement of these single groups under each other. In the history of science, too, names for these single groups are customary before any definite usage as to their systematic arrangement.

Two domains are now, in the first place, distinguished. We require, on the one hand, certain investigations concerning that which *exists;* and, on the other hand, concerning the *value* which we attach to what is actual or to what ought to be. We now see that nothing in relation to its value follows immediately from insight into the origin and continued existence of anything actual whatever; and nothing in relation to the possibility of its being actual follows from insight into its value. Accordingly, al-

though we assume that at the end of the investigation a close connection will be shown between that
which exists and that which is of some value, still,
at the beginning we separate the two investigations,
— the one concerning the actuality and the one concerning the value of things.

§ 5. Of the further organization of the subject,
what follows may be presupposed :

Inducements to questions that concern the explanation of actuality come to us in part from external
nature and in part from the life of the soul. The two
domains do not immediately exhibit the appearance
of complete similarity ; but the consideration of both
leads to a series of quite similar inquiries, — for example, concerning the possibility of the alteration of
one and the same Being, concerning the possibility
of the influence of one Thing upon another, etc.
Such inquiries may be separated from others and
combined into a universal preliminary investigation,
Metaphysic, upon which the Philosophy of Nature
and Psychology should then follow, as applications of
the results reached in it to special cases.

The second main division finds two obviously related subjects in the kinds of value which we ascribe
to the existent, and in those which we ascribe to
such actions or sentiments as *ought* to be ; these are,

however, primarily distinguished by the fact that
only the latter directly include an *obligation*. On
this account, the investigation of the two divides
into Æsthetics and Ethics; and for these two investigations a third, common to both, may be conceived,
but has hitherto never been carried out, — namely,
an investigation concerning the nature of all determinations of value (corresponding to Metaphysic).

SECTION FIRST.

§ 6. In life and in the particular sciences we are constantly employed with the explanation of phenomena which, in the form in which they are presented to us, are full of riddles through their contradictions, gaps, and lack of coherence, — a fact to which allusion has already been made. In doing this we necessarily start from certain general presuppositions to which nature and the coherency of things must correspond in order to be true. These presuppositions are ordinarily employed only in an uncritical way and without any clear consciousness of their meaning; but Metaphysic endeavors to make a collection of them, to explain their true meaning, and to remove the prejudgments which have become attached to them from being accustomed to a limited circle of experience. Three great groups of investigations appear at this point:

1) one, concerning the most general conceptions and propositions which we apply in judging of every actuality;

2) a second, concerning the most general forms

in which this actuality appears in the existences of
nature (Space, Time, Motion) ;

3) a third, concerning the possibility of the 'reciprocal being (*Füreinandersein*) of things,' by which the
one becomes a perceivable object, and the other a
perceiving subject.

These three groups appear under different titles, with
somewhat of deviating limitations and, of course, very
differently treated, in most systems of Metaphysic.

In the Metaphysic of the older school the first
part appears as Ontology ; the second as Cosmology,
having the problem of showing how the individual
things are connected together into an orderly world-
whole, — a problem which, although it is related to
the second of those mentioned above, is still not
identical with it. Rational Psychology corresponds
to the third group. On the contrary, the fourth
part of such Metaphysic, rational theology, must be
distinguished as a constituent of a foreign kind and
not strictly belonging to Metaphysic.

Just so in Herbart's Metaphysic, if we count out
the first part, the 'Methodology', then the others
correspond perfectly to the above-mentioned division : Ontology, Synechology, as the doctrine of
what is permanent, and Eidolology, or the doctrine
of images (εἴδωλα), which arise in one being as coming from the others.

In the same way does Hegel's 'Logic,' by its partition into the doctrines of Being, of Phenomenon
(from which, of course, though to its disadvantage,
space and time remain excluded), and of Idea, exhibit the plainest analogies to the foregoing division
of such problems.

§ 7. Ontology, from its being employed with experience, is led to the following principal inquiries :

1) What, exactly, is the absolute Subject, which
is not a predicate of another ; that is to say, in what
does that consist which is the truly existent in all
'Things,' whose nature we ordinarily believe ourselves able to specify by a number of so-called *properties ;* and which is the *support* (*Träger*) of these
properties and not itself in turn a property of any
other ?

2) How is the possibility of a variety of simultaneous and successive properties belonging to one
and the same subject to be comprehended ?

3) How can such a unity exist among a variety of
Things that the states of one become causes for alterations in the states of another ?

§ 8. Before we consider the different answers
which have been given to these inquiries, we make
prominent some very general kinds of error.

The first is the confounding of the logical analysis
of our mental representations and the metaphysical
explanation of the things to which the mental representations relate. It is in general quite obvious that
there cannot be, in the matter of fact itself and as
developments of its own nature, as many movements
and turnings as would correspond to the various
steps, the separations and combinations, and in general to all the turnings which we must make in
thought, in order from our point of view to apprehend the nature of such matters of fact. This is
perfectly clear to every one, in case one has to do,
for example, with the more intricate artifices of investigation through which we endeavor to discover any
secret fact. Here the whole expenditure of the operations of thought is quite obviously nothing but *our*
subjective exertion, as it were, to get behind the in
itself simple thing. On the contrary, all this becomes obscure, in case one has to do with the simplest
logical operations. And at this point we very generally fall into the error of regarding our logical separations and combinations of the mental images and
their parts as events which happen also in the nature
of the things themselves.

For example ; in definition we premise for the
individual a general conception, and elaborate this
by added modifications up to the point of likeness

with the individual in question. Hence the frequent error, as though in reality some 'primitive animal,' some 'primitive matter,' some 'primitive substance,' must precede as a substratum in fact, from which, as something secondary, the individual subordinate species might originate through the influence of modifying conditions. The logical dependence of the separate members of a classification is, therefore, confounded with a real, matter-of-fact derivation of one from the other.

In *judgment* we divide the object of a perception into a subject, from which we as yet exclude a predicate; then into such predicate; and, finally, into the third mental representation, that of the copula by which the predicate is united again with the subject. These operations are necessary in order to secure clearness to the process of thinking. But it is an error to assume that, in general, any like transaction corresponds to them as a matter of fact, so that there can really be, in the last analysis, a somewhat that is without all predicates, and only just *a* somewhat, but not any *definite* somewhat ; and, further, that there can be predicates which were somewhat previous to their being actualized in some subject; and, finally, that there is in *rerum natura* some 'cement,' as it were, similar to the logical copula by means of which the predicates are brought to 'inhere' — as the customary expression goes — in the subject.

One of the most frequent inducements to such errors as the foregoing lies in the comparisons which we are able at will to establish in the process of thinking between the contents of any two ideas we please. We are very much inclined to regard the predicates — for example, 'greater,' 'smaller,' 'different,' 'opposed,' and the like — which belong 'to the content compared, only *after* the comparison is made, as essential, integrating properties of the content itself.

From these mistakes there originate, in part, a multitude of *artificial* difficulties, inasmuch as we begin to seek for an explanation of matter-of-fact properties of things which we have previously created for them (as, for example, when the question is raised, how an x can be at the same time 'greater' and 'smaller,' — that is, greater than y and smaller than z) : and, in part, many *actual* difficulties are met with and no solution for them found, because we imagine that we have succeeded in exhibiting the development of a matter of fact, when we have in truth merely depicted the development of our conceptions of the matter of fact. To this latter case belongs, for example, the application of the conceptions of 'potentia' and 'actus,' or of 'dynamis'

and 'entelechy,' or of 'power' and 'expression,' —
faults of a kind which is especially frequent in·
ancient philosophy (compare 'Microcosmus,' vol. II,
pp. 321 ff.).

§ 9. A second very general mistake, the exact
opposite of the previous one, consists in the effort to
make clear the supreme principles by explanations
that have no meaning except in the case of individual
phenomena dependent on the principles ; and that
even here have their meaning only in virtue of the
principles themselves. The simplest way of making
this obvious is, in brief, the following.

Our cognition is accustomed to the investigation
of individual events. These have their definite conditions, under which they are produced and maintained. On this account, we can often show step
by step in a pictorial manner, how the phenomenon
arises from the co-operation of its conditions ; that
is to say, we know the mechanism of its coming
to be, the way in which it is produced. Now this
same inquiry may also very easily be raised with
reference to the general principles, which are the
very foundation of the *possibility* of the aforesaid
mechanism, or of every way in which any thing
whatever can be produced. For example, the question is asked, how does it happen that in all

'becoming' one state follows upon the others; or how does a 'cause' begin to produce its appropriate effect. This is as though one should wish to investigate some internal *mechanism*, by which the points of relation existing between these two most general conceptions were held together; although — just the other way — every possible mechanism presupposes the validity of these two conceptions.

It is just so in many other cases. This fault is the opposite of the foregoing, inasmuch as in the case of objects of thought that are absolutely incomprehensible except in the form of abstract concepts and are definable only as to their essential meaning, it is not satisfied with such apprehension as belongs to the concept, but demands for them a kind of intuitive knowledge such as in this case is quite impossible.

§ 10. The difference in different treatises on Metaphysic admits of being referred to two antithetic principles which are dependent on fundamental presuppositions that are together introduced to consideration.

One view, which is *realistic*, finds the inducement to investigation exclusively in the 'contradictions' of experience. If there were none of these, then Realism would take no offence at letting the world pass in the form in which it exists as bare matter of fact; and would raise no further inquiries. Accordingly, if it succeeds in placing underneath this world of experience, a world of what is existent truly and devoid of contradictions, out of which the former becomes comprehensible; then it regards its problems as solved.

The other and *idealistic* view sees in every fact, even although it include no contradiction, some riddle; and it believes that we ought to recognize as truly existent only such matter-of-fact as, by virtue of its meaning and significance, admits of being demonstrated to be an essential member of the rational world-whole.

§ 11. The Metaphysic of Realism is more inclined to the pursuit of special investigations which are attached to single groups of problems; and it is only afterward that it endeavors to combine the results it has attained into one whole. The Metaphysic of Idealism, on the contrary, prefers to apprehend as its single main problem the meaning of the world as a whole; and it believes that the solution of this problem includes that of all the special problems, and that thereby a coherent, uninterrupted development can best be obtained. The *methods* of both partake of this distinction.

Realism takes its point of departure from the absolute certainty of the law of identity. Accordingly, it sees so-called 'contradictions' everywhere that ordinary experience shows us a 'unity of the one and the many' (for example, the 'many properties' of a 'Thing' and their 'alteration'). It further tries to find a general solution for the contradiction in the assertion that the unity is here only *apparent;* and that what corresponds as subject to the many properties (whether simultaneous or successive) is not one Being that remains the same with itself and yet undergoes change, but is a complex of many beings which, in themselves always simple and always self-identical, only appear to us as *one* 'Thing' through their relations to each other and through their changes — as one Thing with many properties, as one changeable thing.

§ **12**. The Metaphysic of Idealism sets itself a single main problem, which is as follows; to discover the nature of the truly Existent, against the recognition of which as absolute, independent, and supreme Ground of actuality, none of those presuppositions which our reason is compelled to make concerning such a principle, any longer protests.

Such a problem leads to a method of its own. That is to say, the aforesaid 'truly Existent,' which we wish to discover, hovers before us, at the beginning of philosophy, in the form of a very obscure although very lifelike presentiment. *Positively*, we are not able exhaustively to express what we mean by it. But yet, in case some thought not identical with it is mentioned to us, we are able very definitely to deny that it is this which we mean. If we therefore assume that we have first established for this obscure content **X** some definition **a**, which contains those features of **X** that are relatively most clear to us; then we can next compare **a** with **X**, and thereupon observe not merely in general that **a** does not perfectly represent what we mean by **X**, but also why or wherein **a** is unlike **X**, and consequently stands in need of improvement. Thus there originates a second definition *a* = **X**, with which the same procedure is instituted as with **a** : and so on, until we finally discover a definition *A* = **X** in which we see all that we obscurely meant under **X** transformed into clear conceptions.

Thus regarded, this method is nothing but a series of subjective operations of thought by which we intend to transform a knowledge of our object which is at first unsatisfactory into one more adequate ; — that is, of operations executed, with an altogether definite purpose in view, by us as interpreting subjects.

If the object **X** still remains as obscure as are those high-flying thoughts called ' the truly Existent,' ' the

Absolute,' etc., then, as a rule, it becomes very difficult to get any altogether accurate consciousness of
the precise reasons why a first definition **a** is not satisfactory. We indeed *feel* its unsatisfactoriness in a
general way, and this of itself urges us toward a second definition *a* which much better corresponds to
the **X**. But the *logical* motives for this transition
remain obscure. It merely follows with a certain
poetic justice ; and now it appears to us, since we
have lost hold of the reins that are to guide the
process of thought, as an inner development peculiar to **X** itself, of which we as thinking subjects
are simply spectators.

On the other hand, Idealism took its point of
departure from the matter-of-fact supposition of a
single Ground of the world, of an 'Absolute,' which
'develops' into the variety of phenomena. If it
had been known *what* this Absolute is, then we
should have been able to deduce from its nature a
mode of development corresponding to it. But this
was not known; on the contrary, the name 'Absolute' merely designated the value of a Supreme Principle to which a content as yet unknown was, so to
speak, to be elevated. No definite mode of development could therefore be divined, but it could simply be asserted what mode may possibly be attributed to the Absolute ; and so in any case it must

at least correspond to the general conception of 'development.'

Now the following thoughts are involved in the foregoing conception, — namely, that the self-developing being *is* not yet that which it is to *become*, but that at the same time the possibility of its becoming this lies in it alone. It therefore appears as a 'germ' which is not yet fully unfolded, but which is 'in itself' what it will later become. Further, the germ must not remain germ, but must develop into a variety of actual phenomena; none of which, although they all correspond perfectly to its essence, is *exclusively* correspondent thereto, without having others beside itself. Therefore that which is 'in itself' (*das An Sich*) is at the same time realized and brought to an end in this development, which is the 'being other than itself'; since it assumes a definite form, and thus excludes other possible forms which it might have assumed. This incongruity between that which the Being is 'in itself' and the 'being other than itself' of the phenomenon must be in turn removed : and it is a further step necessary to the development, by which the one-sidedness of the phenomenon is negated and the Being returns into its own infiniteness; although since it has this definite development behind it, it does not return to the simplicity of Being 'in itself,' but to the higher state of 'Being for self' (*Für-sichsein*).

These three steps deduced from the conception of development *in abstracto* have been established, besides, by many significant examples taken from experience, — as, for example, from vegetable, animal, and spiritual life; and so it came about that the aforesaid primary and subjective method of explaining obscure conceptions blended with this objective 'rhythmus' of development; and philosophy came to believe that it possesses herein a method at once subjective and objective, according to which things have unfolded themselves before our consciousness (compare '*Geschichte der Aesthetik in Deutschland*,' München, 1868, pp. 176–183).

§ 13. It is obvious that, from the foregoing method, there is to be expected only a development in which a certain poetic justice more or less clearly rules; but not such an one as that every step in it can be made good by definite proofs as necessary or as alone possible to the exclusion of others.

In fact, the use of the same method by different philosophers of this school has led to wholly divergent results.

Only the fundamental thought of their Ontology remains; and it is this, that 'Being' is never simple, unchangeable 'Position,' but is constant movement through the three 'Moments' above alluded to, — namely, 'Being-in-itself,' 'Being-other-than-self,' and 'Being-for-self.' It is further agreed that there is only one 'Existent,' whose finite and limited manifestation is the individual things ; and, finally (a fact which may be observed here in a preliminary way), that this one Absolute does not remain a wholly empty name for an obscure point, but has essentially the nature of the Spirit, and its development is the advance from the 'being-in-itself' of unconscious existence to the 'being-for-self' of self-consciousness.

§ 14. The results of Realism are different. Directed primarily toward the explanation of the possibility of phenomena, it naturally required, in opposition to the change which would include a contradiction, that Being should be considered as a simple, irremovable 'position.' It further required, that the primary elements, from whose changeable combination the phenomena proceed, should be seen in a variety of ultimate subjects or real beings. The original nature of these beings it believed cannot be recognized ; but it simply concluded, from the facts that '*appear*,' back to relations which must take place between them in order to make this appearance possible.

Both views, Idealism and Realism, come from different sides on one and the same difficulty. The former can perchance develop, in a general way, from the one Idea which it presupposes, those problems which reality must solve in order to correspond to this Idea. Only it is not able to explain the special actions and reactions which take place between the individual examples of those species of Being that are derived from it ; but for this it needs the 'pluralistic' assumption that the aforesaid Idea, in a manner that requires additional demonstration, has previously divided into a variety of elements which are in the future to act independently.

Realism, on the contrary, in order to comprehend an action and reaction between its many elements, must assume a unity of general laws to which they are all subjected. The explanation of how this subordination of the many under this unity is possible, is the counterpart of the before-mentioned problem of Idealism. We may therefore consider as the final problem of Ontology — a problem not yet satisfactorily solved — this inquiry after the connection between the necessary unity and the alike necessary manifoldness of the Existent.

§ 15. After Ontology has established certain general conceptions of Being, of the Existent, of Hap-

pening and Acting, cosmological investigations raise
the inquiry after the relation of this Being and Acting to Space and Time.   Under this head the principal problems are the following three:

1) The problem whether 'space' exists in itself,
and things are in it, so that the latter are partially
distinguished by their place in space; or whether
space is in things only as a form of intuiting them,
and the latter are accordingly distinguished only
qualitatively, and appear at different points in one
space intuited of them, in consequence of their
qualitative differences toward each other.

Connected with this inquiry after the 'reality' or
'ideal character' of space stands —

2) The inquiry after the nature of 'matter,'
although the two do not coincide.   The question
is: Should the spatial volume of any body of matter
be held to be a continuous volume full of what is
real?   Or is it only a space-volume within which
many active elements exist that are distinguished by
their place but are in themselves unextended?   This
is the question in dispute between the dynamic filling
of space and Atomism, — the meaning of which, however, it appears must be apprehended in a way the
very reverse of what customarily happens.   The
conception of matter as *continuous* asserts that what
is real accomplishes an actual achievement by filling

up space; and, indeed, by filling it up with its presence. The other view allows space to be simply controlled and not 'crammed' full, as it were, by real existence. It alone, besides, would be compatible with the correct view concerning the ideal character of space.

3) A third question in dispute arises from the consideration of what happens in the physical realm. On the one hand, we are necessitated to recognize the origin of phenomena from the co-operation of many previously unconnected elements, and at the same time the validity of general laws according to which these elements act in every case; so that they are dependent for their effect only upon these laws, upon their own permanent nature, and upon the momentary disposition of circumstances, and not at all upon a result which, according to hypothesis, has not as yet been attained. Over against this so-called 'mechanical view' of forces working blindly according to general laws, there stands the idealistic view, which regards only 'active Ideas' as truly effective in the world of things. Such Ideas are ever striving to realize themselves, and on this account are not bound to constantly uniform laws of their action, but modify their mode of behavior at every moment with a teleological reference to the result for which they strive. Now it needs no explanation

to see that, as long as the 'Ideas' use means for their actualization, this actualization cannot follow without certain general laws being valid, in accordance with which these means act. But just so, on the other hand, would the world be absurd if there existed in it *mere* 'mechanism' without any power of Ideas or final purposes. The ultimate object of Cosmology will therefore be the inquiry, how Ideas and final purposes can be effective within a world whose events are subject to the laws of a mechanism.

§ 16. After we have, in Ontology and Cosmology, formed a view concerning the nature of Things and their reciprocal actions, we should in the last part of Metaphysic investigate *Cognition* itself as a single but important case of the reciprocal action between two elements, — to wit, the case in which the one being is capable of apprehending as conscious ideas the impressions which it receives from the others.

In the first place, we should in realistic fashion discover from the consideration of this reciprocal action, that the image of the one being **A** cannot be formed like **A** within the other being **B** ; because, although it always on the one side depends upon the impression from **A**, it likewise on the other side depends on the nature of **B**. This, therefore, is the same as saying that, by virtue of

this unavoidable 'subjectivity of all ideation,' cognition cannot be 'true' in the sense that it copies
the essence of objects in form similar to the objects
themselves; but at most in the sense that it repeats
the relations between things in the form of relations
of their mental images.

The foregoing result, however, causes us to raise
the inquiry of Idealism after the significance of this
entire mode of procedure. The Realism of common
opinion is wont to regard the world, apart from cognition, as a ready-made matter-of-fact that subsists
entirely complete in itself; and cognition as only a
kind of appendage by means of which this subsist-
ing matter-of-fact is simply recapitulated for the
best good of the cognizing being, but without in
this way experiencing any increment of reality.
Now Idealism establishes the truth that the process of ideation itself is one of the most essential constituents of the world's ongoing course;
that objectivity is not a goal the attainment and
further shaping of which is a task set before ideation; but that ideation or, rather, the whole spiritual life is a goal, to the attainment of which is
summoned the entire world of objects that do not
share in the process, and the entire ordering of
relations between them.

§ 17. The design in dividing theoretical Philosophy into Metaphysic and its applications, the Philosophy of Nature and Psychology, is that the first
shall answer the question : How must all that be
which is really to *be* at all ? or, If anything whatever really *is*, to what necessary laws of all thought
is it subjected ? Over against this abstract science
are the two other concrete ones.   That is to say,
they must consider the actuality which, although it
obeys the laws of Metaphysic, still does so in a special form that might be otherwise, and that therefore
is provisionally regarded as only an example, empirically given, of the aforesaid necessary laws of
thought.   But the design of this distinction is neither
accurately carried out, nor does it possess any great
value.

The problem of the Philosophy of Nature would
accordingly be the following; not so much to describe
the elements which are in existence, as rather to
show what general habitudes of action and reaction
occur in this definite ' Nature ' so-called ; and, therefore, what ones among the different forces conceivable
in abstracto actually occur and what ones among the
many possible dispositions of them actually subsist
from the beginning and maintain themselves amid
manifold forms of change.   For example, that the
mass of matter in the world is separated into indi-

vidual material bodies; that these are distinguished
among themselves into cohering and ·reciprocally
exclusive systems; that on our planet the three different forms of inorganic, vegetable, and animal
existence occur; that what exists in these three
kingdoms is — or how far it is — divided into species, kinds, etc.; that a systematic action and reaction, which is necessary for their continued existence, takes place between everything living and the
inorganic material, — all this constitutes the problems of the concrete Philosophy of Nature. From
the realistic point of view, we take an interest in
investigating the effective conditions upon which
all these facts concerning the ordering of nature depend; from the idealistic, in showing that it is an
ordering in which, if one knows it once for all, the
striving after the fulfilment of those universal problems that are unavoidable in every conceivable rational
world may be recognized again and again.   But Idealism claims far too much when it, as in Schelling's
philosophy of nature, aims to ' deduce' all these concrete forms of existence, as consequences necessary
to thought, from one Supreme Idea.

§ 18. In Psychology, too, the same principal views
stand in contrast with one other.   The realistic aims
by investigations in causality to discover the condi-

tions under which every single phenomenon of the life of the Soul occurs, endures, or changes, and by reciprocal action with other phenomena lays the foundation for new states. Such investigations may either be founded, in a manner quite like that of natural science, upon experience and experiment, or philosophically upon metaphysical presuppositions. The larger gain with reference to the explanation of the individual comes in the former way ; but a more secure apprehension for the whole of a theory is only to be gained in the second way. But the entire realistic investigation is indispensable, because it is only the knowledge of the working forces in the life of the Soul which admits of practical applications, — in Pædagogics, Psychiatry, etc.

Idealism also upon this point investigates, in the first place, the constitutive conception of the Soul, — that is to say, the special Idea for the realization of which the Soul is summoned to a definite place in the whole coherent system of the world ; and it then aims at demonstrating the individual activities of the Soul as a cohering series of steps of development, which gradually construct for this conception an ever more adequate realization. The previous attempts (Schelling, Hegel, etc.) suffer, in part, from inaccuracies to which the previous article alludes, and, in part, from an over-estimate (that is without sufficient *motif*) of mere intelligence in comparison with the *whole* spiritual life. They look upon mere self-knowledge, the most perfect self-consciousness, as the final goal of the Soul and of the World ; while in our view all intelligence is only the *conditio sine qua non*, under which alone the final purposes that are really supreme — personal love and hate, the moral culture of character — and, in general, the whole content of life so far as it has value appears possible at all.

SECTION SECOND.

PRACTICAL PHILOSOPHY.

§ **19**. Realism takes up those claims, of the *conscience* that obligates us to a definite form of conduct, which urge themselves upon our interior life, as though they were mere problems of fact, — problems on this account because, in spite of the clearness with which the claims of conscience follow in many individual cases, still in other cases we feel ourselves obligated in a contradictory fashion to irreconcilable modes of conduct.

Investigation, accordingly, proceeds in the first place to the confirming of the matter of fact, — that is to say, to establishing certain fundamental moral principles in which, since they refer to the most simple relations of several personal wills toward one another, a uniformly similar and unchangeable judgment of approbation or disapprobation is expressed concerning a definite mode of the will's behavior. Whence these judgments of conscience originate within us; in what connection they stand with the laws that govern what happens in reality; whether, finally, they admit of being deduced from one supreme command or not, — all these are allied questions, the answer to which, however it may turn out, neither heightens nor diminishes the *obligatory* force of the aforesaid moral principles.

Realism pronounces it to be a capital fault to surrender this independence of the moral principles, and to be willing to deduce the supreme rules, according to which our conduct has to be directed, from any theoretical insight whatever into the nature of reality. In 'Being' alone no significance with respect to what 'ought' to be is involved. From that which is and happens, prudential maxims for conduct which will shun the dangers of this reality admit of being developed ; but not the obligations which, apart from any consequences, make any kind of conduct appear *in itself* valuable, honorable, and praiseworthy.

The investigations of Idealism have, for the most part, justified these observations. Since it takes its point of starting from a supreme fact, — to wit, the development of the absolute 'Ground' of the world, — it has not discovered, strictly speaking, any place for the conception of such an obligatory 'ought' ; but it substitutes for the conceptions of the morally 'Good,' and the morally 'Bad,' simply certain theoretical conceptions of the harmonizing or not-harmonizing of any mode of conduct with the *tendency* of the self-development of the Absolute.

§ **20.** The *formal* distinction between the two modes of treatment consists in this, that the realistic proceeds from general laws of conduct, from which the special maxims of conduct that are necessary in consideration of the circumstances can be deduced for each particular case of an occasion for conduct ; and from which, besides, since it brings into consideration the empirical nature of man and the ever recurring social relations, science is also able to develop a series of permanent life-aims that hold good both for the individual and for society. This last problem may be called that of 'Practical Philosophy' in special ; while the doctrine of the culture of character according to general ethical principles is called 'Moral Science' or 'Ethics.'

Idealism, as a rule, does not reach any special distinction in these two forms of 'discipline.' To it the 'Good' appears, not as that which merely *ought* to be, but likewise as that which eternally *is*. As well the individual man as society and the history of society are, in its view, 'factors in the development of the Absolute.' To it that appears as 'good,' which adapts itself to the meaning of this development.

SECTION THIRD.

§ **21.** A common conclusion for both theoretical and practical investigations in philosophy is sought for in the Philosophy of Religion.

We designate this part of philosophy by this name, because the human mind has uniformly sought in *religion* for such a conclusion to its view of the world; that is to say, for certainty concerning the final and supreme Cause of that reality, of which every individual investigation, since it proceeds from limited points of view, gives only a one-sided explanation. More particularly, however, this certainty has reference to the inquiry, how it is that what appears in our conscience as the only thing that has real value, — how the Good and the Beautiful possess a validity corresponding to their value in the totality of the world. Finally, we employ the term, because the human mind has sought for a supplement to our experience of the world, that shall follow from the results of such painstaking endeavors, by means of some intuition of a supersensible extension of the world into realms withdrawn from experience.

It is in 'Religion' that the human mind has either solved all these problems by a lively phantasy, or some revelation has furnished the solution. In the first case, philosophy has to explain, to test, and to correct, the impulses by which the phantasy would be directed. In the second case, it has to demonstrate, to what demands of the mind, that are in themselves justifiable, the revelation vouchsafes a satisfaction which is not discoverable by the reason, but which is intelligible as soon as it exists.

But even apart from this relation to religion as a fact actually met with, philosophy carries within itself the very greatest demand for reflection upon the connection between its theoretical and its ethical view of the world.

§ 22. Should the before-mentioned problem be completely solved, then the 'Philosophy of Religion' would be in a position to make the transition from the way of investigation to the way of a continuous, systematic exhibition of philosophical truth; since it would indeed have fused all the results of investigation into a single unity.

But at this point philosophy concludes with an unattainable ideal : — that is to say, with the conviction that the universal and necessary laws of thought, in accordance with which we judge of all

reality; second, that the primitive facts of this
reality; third, that the supreme Ideas of the Good
and the Beautiful, which hover before us as the
final purposes of the world, — are all perfectly
coherent factors of one and the same Supreme
Principle, of the nature of God, although we are
unable strictly to demonstrate this fact of their
coherency. From the fact that such general laws
hold good in mathematics, it does not follow that
this system of nature which is empirically given
is necessary, and any other is impossible. Both
the laws and the facts appear to us possible and
valid, even although no Idea of the Good were
ruling the world. In brief, laws, facts, and final
purposes (Ideas) are *for us* three principles, distinct from each other, and not deducible from each
other.

For this reason Philosophy can never be such an
unchanging science, as to be able to deduce from
one Supreme Principle all its results in uniform
sequence; but its investigations will always be separated into (1) those of Metaphysic, which concern the possibility of the world's course ; (2) into
those of the Philosophy of Nature, which concern
the connection, in fact, of its reality; and (3) into
those of the Philosophy of Religion, which concern
its ideal significance and final purposes.